Belle & Boo

S

IS FOR

Sewing

Illustrations by Mandy Sutcliffe
Photography by Laura Edwards

QUADRILLE

Contents

This is Belle, and this is Boo.
They are always together –
on sunny days,
rainy days,
and dreamy let's-be-lazy days.

Welcome to the make-believe world of Belle and Boo, an enchanted place where the children and animal characters created by illustrator Mandy Sutcliffe live blissfully side by side. With this book of over 25 projects to make for children, you too can now inhabit the magical world of Belle and Boo and bring its unique qualities of warmth, innocence and adventure to your own family life.

Designed to engage their imaginations, the projects to sew in this book will transport your little ones to magical realms, such as the far-flung oceans with the Treasure Island Map on page 62, a play mat that holds hidden riches in a treasure-chest purse, and Ava's Play Tent on page 12, a secret hideaway that makes perfect den for any day-dreaming princess. Belle's Bakery on page 28 is stocked with yummy cupcakes, biscuits and carrots, all handstitched from felt, that can be traded for the Belle & Boo coins that are copied and coloured from the templates provided. Playing shop is the perfect way to introduce basic numeracy skills, whilst making maths fun.

As well as her companion and confidant Boo, Belle has many other toy and animal friends. With the instructions on pages 92–97, you can bring to life to your very own version of Honey Bear, a classic teddy with jointed, moveable arms and legs. Or sew a Pullalong Duck, a characterful miniature duck, which you can find on page 18. Perhaps best of all, there is the Rag Doll on page 44, a charming, traditional cloth doll that has a wardrobe of outfits to make too.

For those out-and-about days spent taking a nature walk through your local park, make your little scamps their own Woodland Masks on pages 84–89 from wool felt, and take turns pretending to be the fox, owl, deer or squirrel. Cutting out simple felt shapes is a good starter project for a young crafter, so why not set your child the task of cutting out all the pieces of the either the Woodland

Masks or the handpuppets for the Puppet Show on pages 54–61, while you tackle the slightly trickier sewing parts. With the puppet theatre and the Belle and Boo handpuppets, you child and their friends can reaact their favourite Belle & Boo stories, or event their own fantastical tales.

For those who are keen to learn new sewing skills, or for anyone who needs a refresher, full instructions are given for the techniques used in the projects on pages 120–123. But you don't have to be an expert stitcher to make all the projects in this book. Some of the ideas involve no more than some cutting, so even if you have never threaded a needle before you can still make the exquisite Felt Forest on page 74. You can build a picture again and again with the felt shapes, telling a different, enchanting story each time. The Christmas Ornaments on pages 110–113 involve no real sewing at all, just some cutting and threading of ribbon, but we love the festive salt-dough shapes so much that we just had to include them.

The creative and inspirational projects in this book will warm your heart and help you to craft a magical world to share with your child, creating something far more valuable than you can ever imagine – a wealth of shared memories for you both to treasure always.

Love,
Belle &
Boo x

Belle & Boo
PROJECTS

In this section you will find a collection of charming projects to make for your special little one. Inspired by the sweetly nostalgic world of Belle & Boo, the collection of over 25 original items includes soft toys, inventive play spaces and dress-up ideas. Create everlasting memories for you and your children with this captivating selection of creative playtime projects.

Ava's Play Tent

145 x 200cm each of two cotton fabrics in complementary prints, one in dark pink, one in pale pink

135cm cotton tape, 2cm wide

Nine D-rings, 2cm in diameter

220cm bobble fringing

One plastic hula hoop, 65cm in diameter

50cm thin cord or shoelace, 3mm in diameter

150cm cotton tape, thick cord or strong string for hanging

12cm diameter disc of thick card with small hole at the centre

Curtain ring

Nine tent pegs or twigs

Large bead or button

Matching sewing thread

Sewing machine

Basic sewing kit

SIZE
One size, approximately 140cm tall

CUTTING OUT
The binding strips and panels are all 145cm long, so instead of cutting them out with dressmaking shears you can simply mark the widths along the selvedge and tear the fabric along the grain.

Two binding strips, one in each colour fabric: Tear off the raw edges of the fabric to square them off. Snip into the selvedge, 5cm from the edge and across the width.

Eight tent panels, four in each colour fabric: Fold the remaining fabric in half lengthways, and then into quarters, again lengthways. Snip into the selvedge at the three folds and tear across the fabric to give four panels in each fabric, each approximately 145 x 47.5cm.

BINDING THE OPEN EDGES
1 Press under a 1cm turning along one long edge of each binding strip. With raw edges aligning and right sides facing, pin a dark pink binding strip to a light pink tent panel. Machine stitch 1cm from the edge and press the seam allowance over the binding. Turn the binding strip to the back, so that the fold just overlaps the stitch line. Pin, tack and machine stitch down. Repeat with a light pink binding strip and a dark pink tent panel.

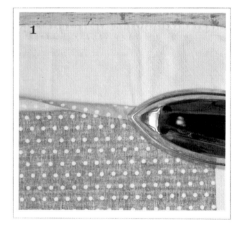

SEWING THE PANELS

2 Alternating the light and dark fabrics, and with the binding at the outside edges, sew the tent panels together with enclosed seams. Pin the long edges together with wrong sides facing and machine stitch, taking a 6mm seam allowance. Press the seams open, then re-fold so that the right sides are facing. Press each seam flat. Machine stitch, taking a 1cm seam allowance. Press the double hem to one side and stitch it down from the front.

ADDING THE ANCHOR LOOPS

3 Turn under a double 15mm hem along the bottom edge of the joined tent panels. Cut the cotton tape into nine 15cm lengths. Thread one length of tape through a D-ring, fold back the raw edges and pin the tape loop to one bottom corner. Machine stitch all along the hem to secure both the hem and the loops in place. Add the other tape loops at the end of each of the seam lines and the second corner.

JOINING THE ROOF

4 Press a 5cm turning along the top edge of the tent panels for the drawstring channel. Pin and stitch this down. Insert a pin at each side edge, 45cm down from each top corner. With right side inwards, fold the tent so that the pins line up. Pin the side edges together from this point up to the top corner. Machine stitch, taking a 4cm seam allowance. Press the seam open.

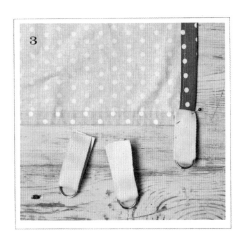

ADDING THE BOBBLES

5 Trim the edges of the tent opening with a length of bobble fringing. Pin and tack the tape part of the fringing to the wrong side, so the bobbles just peep over the top. Fold back a 1cm turning at each end and machine stitch in place.

FIXING THE TEN TO THE HOOP

6 Turn back and press down a 40cm turning around the top edge. Drape the tent over the plastic hula hoop, so that the crease lies along the top edge. Starting at the front opening, enclose the hoop by hand sewing the front and back of the fabric together with a line of long running stitches (see page 123).

GATHERING THE ROOF

7 Cut a small notch across the top of the front seam. Fix a safety pin to one end of the cord or shoelace and pin the other end close to the notch. Thread the cord all the way through the drawstring channel, then draw it up and knot tightly. Trim the ends back to 3cm, then push the knot and the ends back inside the opening.

ADDING THE HANGING LOOP

8 Thread the remaining thin cord or shoelace through the curtain ring. Pass the ends through the top of the tent. Working from the inside, pass both ends through the hole in the cardboard disc and then thread one of the ends through the bead or button. Pull up the cord and knot securely.

PUTTING UP THE TENT

9 To hang the tent, tie a loop of cotton tape or strong string through the curtain ring and knot it securely to an overhead tree branch. You will need nine tent pegs or twigs, one for each cotton loop. Bang the pegs or twigs into the ground with a mallet to hold the tent in place.

Pullalong Duck

Our duck is stitched in a contrasting thread so that the seam lines are clear, but you should use a thread that matches the colour of your fabric.

30 x 35cm fleece fabric in yellow
10 x 5cm thick felt in orange
Safety-standard polyester toy filling
10 x 15cm medium-weight card
Two black beads or small buttons,
  6mm in diameter
Matching sewing thread
Sewing machine
Basic sewing kit

For the trolley
Wheeled platform or
Four long nails with flat heads
Four 3cm toy wheels or wooden discs
  with central holes
Wood glue
Two lengths of wood, each 6 x 1.5 x 1.5cm
  (for the axles)
Two lengths of wood, each 6 x 1.5 x 1.2cm
Rectangle of wood, 6 x 20 x 1.2cm
One small screw eye
1m of string
Hot glue gun

Templates: Pullalong Duck on page 124

SIZE
One size, approximately 18 x 14 x 10cm
(without wheels)

CUTTING OUT
from fleece fabric
  two bodies, one reversed
  two wings, one reversed
  two bases, one reversed
from felt fabric
  one upper beak
  one lower beak
from card
  one card base

CUTTING GUIDE

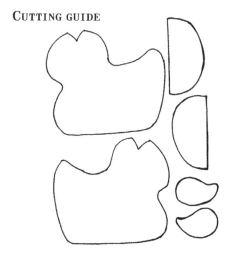

SAFETY FIRST: *This is a toy for a toddler. If this is being given to a younger child do not sew on eyes, but instead mark with a fabric pen. Also, make sure you are there to supervise whilst the child is playing as the string may tangle.*

MARKING UP THE PIECES
Using an air-erasable fabric pen, transfer the markings for the eye, beak and wing positions to both body pieces.

SEAMS
The seam allowance is 6mm throughout. Mark the stitch line on each piece, 6mm from the edge, using a ruler and an air-erasable fabric pen.

Reinforce both ends of each seam with two or three stitches worked in the reverse direction.

MAKING UP THE HEAD
1 With right sides facing, pin and tack the small head dart, matching points A. Machine stitch. Repeat on the other body piece.

ADDING THE WINGS
2 Cut a 2cm slit inside both wing outlines. Pin and tack the wings in place on both bodies, with the right sides facing upwards. Machine stitch all the way round, 3mm from the outside edge.

3 Firmly stuff the wing with toy filling through the slit. Use the blunt end of a pencil to push the fibres right to the tip.

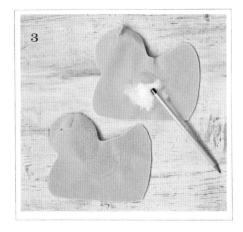

MAKING UP THE BODY

4 With right sides facing, pin the two bodies together. When you reach the head darts, fold one seam allowance to the left and the other to the right, so that they butt up neatly. Tack between points A and B, leaving the base open, then machine stitch 6mm from the edge. Trim the seam allowance back to 3mm.

JOINING ON THE BASE

5 With right sides facing, pin and tack the two halves of the base together along the straight edge. Sew a 2cm seam at each end, taking a 6mm seam allowance and leaving a long gap in the middle. Fold back and tack the seam allowance on each side of the gap.

6 Pin the base to the body, matching points A and B. Tack the edges together, easing the fabric so that they fit neatly together. With the body uppermost, machine stitch all round the base. Trim the seam allowance back to 3mm. Turn right side out and firmly stuff with toy filling. Slip the cardboard base through the opening, then close the gap with small slip stitches.

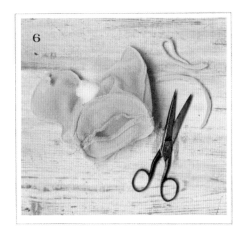

TROLLEY: *We used the base of an old wooden truck to make the pullalong base for the duck, but you can follow the instructions on the right to make a similar one. Alternatively, look in the toy box for an old toy, which can be upcycled and repainted.*

ADDING THE FINISHING TOUCHES

7 Sew the eyes securely in place using a double length of thread or draw them on using a fabric pen. Using orange thread, sew the lower beak to the bottom half of the guide line and the upper beak to the top half. Fix the duck securely to the wheeled platform using a hot glue gun.

MAKING THE TROLLEY

8 Nail a wheel to each end of the two 6 x 1.5 x 1.5cm wooden axles. Glue the two 6 x 1.5 x 1.2cm lengths of wood flush against the short ends of the large wooden rectangle base, then glue the axles next to them, underneath the base. When dry, sand lightly and paint if you like. Fix the screw eye to the middle of one end of the base and tie on the string. Use a glue gun to fix the base of the duck to the top of the trolley.

Egg Hunt Bag

For the bag
60 x 30cm each of two cotton fabrics in
    coordinating prints
60 x 30cm calico (if you are using light-
    weight fabric for the outer bag)
120cm bias binding, 2cm wide
60cm woven cotton tape, 2cm wide
Matching sewing thread
Sewing machine
Basic sewing kit

For the eggs
Wooden eggs
Acrylic craft paints
Paintbrushes

SIZE
One size, approximately 14 x 12 x 10cm

CUTTING OUT
from main fabric
    two 25 x 20cm rectangles
from contrast fabric
    two 25 x 20cm rectangles
from calico
    two 25 x 20cm rectangles
Cut a 5cm square from the two bottom
corners of each fabric piece.

SEAMS
The seam allowance is 1cm throughout.

Reinforce both ends of each seam with
two or three stitches worked in the
reverse direction.

SEWING UP THE MAIN BAG
1 If you are using calico to give extra body
to your bag, pin one piece to the wrong
side of each main fabric piece. Place all
four fabric layers together, with right
sides facing, then pin and machine stitch
along the side and bottom edges. Press the
seams open.

2 Open out and then re-fold the bottom
corners so that the seam lines meet at
the centre. Pin the edges together and
machine stitch. Press the seams open and
turn the main bag right side out.

MAKING THE BAG LINING

3 Make up the lining from the coordinating print fabric in the same way as the main bag and slip it inside, with wrong sides together. Match up the seam lines, then pin and tack the main bag and the lining together around the top edge.

BINDING THE OPENING

4 Neaten the top edge of the bag with a round of bias binding (see page 122). Open out the top fold, overlap the end and pin it to the left of a seam line. Pin the bias binding all the way round the top edge of the bag and trim the end, leaving a 1cm overlap. Tack, then machine stitch along the open fold line. Turn the other edge to the inside of the bag and then pin down and slip stitch along the folded edge.

MAKING THE BAG HANDLES

5 Cut the woven cotton tape into two 30cm lengths. Cut two 32cm lengths of bias binding. Pin the bias binding over the cotton tape so that there is a 1cm overlap at each end. Tack down, folding back the ends neatly. Machine stitch all the way around the tape, 3mm from the edge. Make the second handle in the same way.

6 Mark a point 6cm in from each corner with a pin. Sew the bag handles securely in place by hand, lining up the outside corners with the pins.

PAINTING THE EGGS

7 You can now have fun decorating the eggs. Cover each egg with two layers of acrylic craft paint in a single colour. Next, add the details with a fine paintbrush. Make up your own designs or follow Belle's patterns on this page.

Belle's Bakery

YOU WILL NEED

for each cupcake
20 x 3cm corduroy or other ribbed fabric
   in white
7cm circle of felt in white
11cm circle of cotton fabric in beige

for the cupcake toppings
Scraps of felt in the following colours:
   dark pink, light pink, brown, lemon,
   white, orange and green
Cotton embroidery thread in the following
   colours: blue, yellow and red

for each gingerbread Boo biscuit
12 x 6cm thick felt in mid brown
Cotton embroidery thread in white

for each jam biscuit
15 x 8cm thick felt in light brown
7cm square of felt in red and cream

for each carrot
10cm square of felt in orange
6 x 5cm felt in green
Dark orange waterproof felt-tip pen

for the coins
Gold crayon or felt-tip pen
Thin card

Fabric glue
Safety-standard polyester toy filling
Basic sewing kit

Templates: cupcake toppings, icing, star,
   petal, leaf, gingerbread Boo, carrot and
   coins on page 125

MAKING THE CUPCAKE WRAPPERS

1 Neaten one long edge of the white corduroy or ribbed fabric strip with a zigzag stitch. Join the short ends with a narrow seam to make a continuous loop. With the wrong side and seam facing outwards, pin and tack the circle of white felt to one long raw edge. Machine stitch, taking a 4mm seam allowance. Turn right side out.

ADDING THE CUPCAKE TOPPINGS

2 Set your sewing machine to a long straight stitch and sew around the outside edge of the beige cotton fabric circle. These are your gathering stitches. Using the template, cut out the icing from coloured felt and fix it to the centre of the beige circle with fabric glue. Now have fun adding the cupcake toppings.

3 For the cupcake with sprinkles topping, cut the icing from pink felt. Next, to make the sprinkles, embroider a scattering of short straight stitches (see page 120), using four strands of cotton embroidery thread in blue, yellow and red.

4 For the cupcake with a star, cut the icing from white, pink or yellow felt. Using the template, cut out a star from lemon or orange felt and glue this to the centre of the icing. Mark seven or eight evenly spaced dots around the star and work a large French knot on each one, using all six strands of cotton embroidery thread.

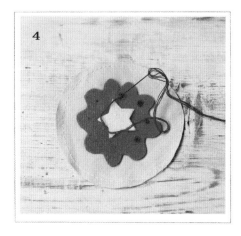

5 The chocolate brown icing is topped with a buttercup. Using the template, cut five petals from lemon felt and one leaf from green felt. Sew the leaf to the centre of the icing. Stitch the petals together on a single length of thread, making a small pleat at the bottom of each one, then pull up tightly. Stitch the petals to the icing and embroider a cluster of yellow French knots over the centre join.

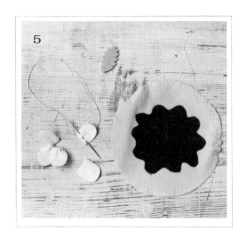

ASSEMBLING THE CUPCAKES
6 Gently pull up the gathering stitches on the beige cotton fabric circle, distributing the folds evenly so that you have a domed cupcake shape. Stuff lightly with toy filling, then add more toy filling to the white cupcake wrapper. Pin the cupcake inside the wrapper and slip stitch them together around the top edge of the wrapper.

MAKING THE BOO GINGERBREAD
7 Using the template, cut out the Boo silhouette from thick brown felt. Embroider his eye and tail with ovals of satin stitch (see page 121), using four strands of white cotton embroidery thread.

MAKING THE JAM BISCUITS
8 Cut 6cm circles from both the red and cream felt. Draw two 6cm circles on the brown felt and cut around the outside edge with scalloped scissors. Fold one of the brown felt circles in half and cut a half-heart shape from the centre. Sandwich the four layers, fixing them together with a glue stick. Stick the cream circle onto the solid brown circle, then add the red circle and finally the brown circle with the heart cutout.

MAKING THE CARROTS

9 Fold the carrot shape in half lengthways and stitch the long straight edges together, taking a 6mm seam allowance. Trim back the seam allowance at both ends, then turn right side out. Sew a line of small running stitches around the curved top edge. Lightly stuff the carrot with toy filling.

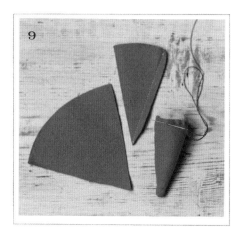

11 Add texture to the carrot by working short straight stitches in brown thread all along it, then drawing on a few extra lines using a dark orange felt-tip pen.

10 Snip a row of long thin triangles into one long edge of the green felt, then roll it up to make the carrot top. Hold it together by stitching through the base, then tuck it into the top of the carrot. Draw up the gathering thread and secure with a few stitches.

MAKING THE COINS

12 Photocopy the coin outlines on page 125 and colour each one in using a gold crayon or felt-tip pen. Roughly cut out all of the coin 'heads' and stick them onto thin card. Cut neatly around the outlines. Next, cut out the coin 'tails' and stick them to the reverse side of the 'heads'.

Painter's Smock

YOU WILL NEED

120 x 70cm plain cotton chambray fabric,
    for the smock
30 x 20cm print cotton fabric, for the
    pockets
150cm bias binding, 12mm wide
One button
Matching cotton embroidery thread,
    for the hand-stitched button loop
Matching sewing thread
Sewing machine
Basic sewing kit

Template: Painter's smock (see page 126)

SIZE
One size, to fit a 5–6 year old
Length from shoulder to hem:
    approximately 55cm
Measurement around chest:
    approximately 60cm

PREPARING THE PATTERN PIECES
Enlarge the templates for the painter's
smock and pocket on page 126 by 250%,
using a photocopier.

CUTTING OUT
from cotton chambray
    one front, cut on the fold as indicated
    two backs, one reversed
from print cotton
    two pockets

PREPARING THE SMOCK PIECES
1 Neaten each of the side and shoulder
edges of the front and back smock pieces
with a zigzag or overlocking stitch.
Following the markings on the paper
pattern and using an air-erasable pen,
transfer the neck pleat lines and the
positions of the two pockets onto the front
smock piece.

STITCHING THE POCKETS

2 Neaten the top edges of both pockets with a 1cm double hem (see page 122). Press back a 1cm turning along the side and bottom edges of the pockets, then press back 1cm at each bottom corner.

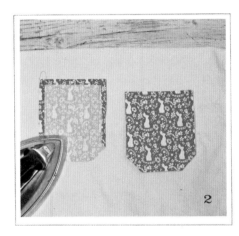

3 Following the pocket position markings, pin the two pockets in place on the smock front. Tack and then machine stitch them in place, 3mm from the folded edges.

PLEATING THE CENTRE FRONT

4 Fold the left-hand pleat line (A) inwards so that it lies along the centre pleat line (B). Pin it in place, then tack through all the layers, along the folds and neck edge to keep it securely in place. Do the same with the right-hand pleat line (A) to make a double pleat.

JOINING THE BACK PIECES

5 Place the two back smock pieces together, with right sides facing, matching up all the raw edges. Mark a point 20cm down from the neck, then pin the two pieces together between the marked point and the hem. Tack and then machine stitch, taking a 2cm seam allowance. Press the seam open, then press back a 2cm turning along both sides of the top opening.

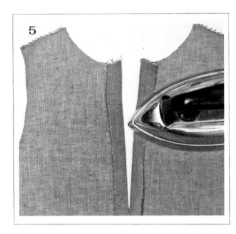

6 Working from the right side, stitch down the left turning, 5mm from the inside edge. When you reach the end, turn the fabric through 90 degrees and sew 1cm across the seam. Reinforce the opening by sewing backwards and then forwards again, then sew down the right turning. Trim off the top 5mm at each side of the neck edge to give a smooth curve.

JOINING THE FRONT AND BACK

7 With the right sides facing inwards, pin the front and back together at the shoulder and side edges. Machine stitch, taking a 1cm seam allowance, then press all four seams open. Turn the smock right side out.

BINDING THE NECK & ARMHOLES

8 Neaten the neck edge of the smock with a round of bias binding (see page 122). Leaving a 1cm overlap, open out one folded edge of the bias binding. Matching the raw edges, tack the bias binding all round the neck edge, stretching it slightly so that it fits comfortably around the curve. Trim the end, leaving a 1cm overlap. Machine stitch along the open fold line, then trim and tuck in the raw end. Turn the other edge of the binding over to the reverse and tack it down. Slip stitch along the folded edge, just inside the stitch line.

9 Open out one edge of the binding as for the neck and fold back a 1cm turning. Tack the fold in line with the underarm seam, then tack the binding all round the armhole edge, stretching it to fit. Trim the end, leaving a 1cm overlap. Machine stitch along the open fold line, then turn the other edge of the binding over to the reverse and tack it down. Slip stitch along the folded edge.

ADDING THE FASTENING

10 Make a hand-stitched button loop (see page 121) or a machine-stitched buttonhole on one side of the neck edge. Sew the button securely on the opposite edge to the button loop or buttonhole.

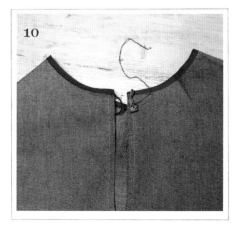

SEWING THE HEM

11 Turn under and press a double hem all around the bottom edge of the smock (see page 122) and machine stitch in place.

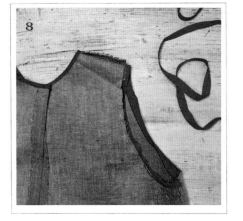

Rag Doll

YOU WILL NEED

70 x 50cm plain cotton fabric, for the doll
25 x 15cm pink gingham cotton fabric,
    for the knickers
Knitting needle
Safety-standard polyester toy filling
50g ball wool yarn, in double-knitting
    weight, for the hair
20 x 20cm square of card
50cm narrow ribbon
Cotton embroidery thread in black and
    red, for the features
Pink colouring crayon
Matching sewing thread
Sewing machine
Basic sewing kit

for the summer dress
60 x 45cm pink gingham cotton
Narrow elastic
Bodkin or small safety pin
Two 12mm buttons
Cotton embroidery thread in pink
Matching sewing thread

for the shoes
30 x 15cm dark grey felt
20 x 10cm light grey felt
Matching sewing thread
Two 12mm buttons

for the top & skirt
50 x 20cm cotton fabric in a plain colour
60 x 20cm cotton fabric in a coordinating
    print
Narrow elastic
Bodkin or small safety pin
Matching cotton embroidery thread
One 12mm button

Templates for the doll: face, back head,
    front body, back body, arm, leg and sole
    on pages 127 and 128
Templates for the summer dress: front
    knickers, back knickers, front yoke,
    back yoke, sleeve and facing on pages
    127–129
Templates for the shoes: uppers and sole
    on page 129
Templates for the top: front and back
    on page 129

SIZE
One size: approximately 50cm tall

PREPARING THE PATTERN PIECES
Enlarge the templates on pages 127–129
by 150%, using a photocopier, and cut out.

CUTTING OUT
from plain cotton fabric
    one face
    two back heads
    one front body
    two back bodies, one reversed
    four arms, two reversed
    four legs, two reversed
    two soles
from gingham cotton fabric
    one front knickers
    two back knickers

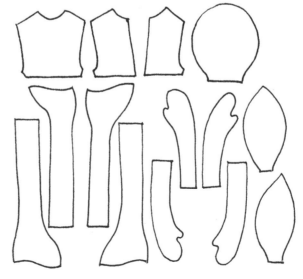

CUTTING GUIDE
Plain fabric

MARKING UP THE RAG DOLL PIECES

Using an air-erasable fabric pen, transfer the markings for the centre front and back of the sole, points D and F.

SEAMS

The seam allowance is 6mm throughout. Mark the stitch line on each piece, 6mm from the edge, using a ruler and an air-erasable fabric pen.

Reinforce both ends of each seam with two or three stitches worked in the reverse direction.

MAKING UP THE ARMS

1 Pin and tack two arm pieces together. Machine stitch from points A to B. Trim the seam allowance back to 3–4mm. Turn right side out and gently ease out the seams using a knitting needle. Stuff with toy filling to within 2cm of the top edge. Machine stitch across the top of the arm, 6mm from the edge. Make the second arm in the same way.

MAKING UP THE LEGS

2 Pin and tack two leg pieces together. Machine stitch the sides together, from points C to D and E to F, leaving the top and bottom edges open. Trim the seam allowance back to 3–4mm. Cut a series of 4mm snips along the bottom foot edge, spacing them 8–10mm apart.

Matching points D and F, pin the front and back of a sole to the bottom of the leg. Gently stretching the snips, pin the rest of the sole all round the foot edge. Tack in place, then machine stitch, with the leg uppermost. Turn right side out and gently ease out the seams. Stuff with toy filling to within 3mm of the top edge. Matching the front and back seams at the centre, machine stitch across the top of the leg, 6mm from the edge. Make the second leg in the same way.

MAKING UP THE BODY

3 With right sides facing, pin and tack the small centre darts in the front body and front knickers. Machine stitch. Next, sew the two together along the waistline, with the right sides facing inwards. Press the seam over the gingham.

With right sides facing, pin and tack the small darts in the two back knickers. Machine stitch. Next, join them to the two back pieces along the waistline, with the right sides facing inwards. Press the seams over the gingham. Sew the two completed back pieces together along the centre back seam and press the seam open.

MAKING UP THE HEAD

4 Draw the eyes and mouth onto the face piece using an air-erasable fabric pen. Stitch the two small darts at the top and neck edges. Stitch the two back heads together along the centre back seam. Cut a series of 4mm snips all round the neck edge of the front and back heads, as you did for the foot edge. Easing the snips around the curve, pin, tack and stitch the front head to the front body and the back head to the back body. Press the seam downwards.

JOINING THE FRONT AND BACK

5 Pin and tack the front and back together and machine stitch around the shoulders and head, between points G. Seam along both sides, from points H to I. Press back the seam allowance all round, including along the unstitched armholes and bottom edge. Turn right side out and stuff firmly with toy filling.

ADDING THE LIMBS

6 Tuck the raw top edges of the arms into the armholes and hand sew them securely in place with several rounds of small slip stitches. Attach the legs in the same way, placing one leg at each end of the opening, then slip stitch all the way along to close the gap.

ADDING THE HAIR

7 Wind half of the wool yarn around the card and cut along the centre to make the strands of hair. Taking three or four strands at a time, fold them in half. Using matching thread, back stitch them along the centre of the head, from the front dart to 2cm above the back neck. Tie the wool hair into two bunches, securing with coloured ribbon ties, then trim the ends to neaten. Stitch the ribbon ties to the sides of the head to keep them in place.

Embroidering the Features

8 Using two strands of black cotton embroidery thread, work the eyes in satin stitch. Using two strands of red cotton embroidery thread, work the mouth in back stitch (see page 121). Add blush to the cheeks using a pink colouring crayon.

Summer Dress

Cutting Out

from gingham cotton fabric

    one front yoke
    two back yokes
    two sleeves
    one facing
    one 45 x 15cm rectangle, for the skirt

Making up the Bodice

9 Join the front and back yokes at the shoulder seams, then press the seam allowances towards the back. With right sides facing, pin the facing around the neck and stitch all round the inside edge. Trim the seam allowance back to 3mm. Turn the facing to the wrong side of the bodice and press.

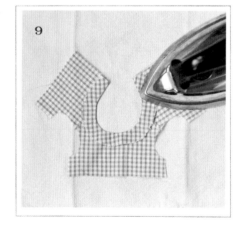

Sewing in the Sleeves

10 Mark the centre top of both sleeves. Zigzag the bottom edges, then press back and unfold a 1cm hem. Machine stitch a line of long, straight gathering stitches between the two points A on the sleevehead. With right sides facing, pin a sleeve to one armhole, matching the corners and the centre top. Pull up one of the threads to gather the sleevehead. Adjust the gathers so that they lie evenly. Pin, tack and machine stitch in place, then trim the seam allowance and zigzag to neaten. Add the other sleeve in the same way. Fold back the turning at the cuff and slip stitch down, leaving a 6mm gap in the seam. Fix a bodkin or small safety pin to the elastic and feed it through the gap and all round the hem. Draw up to make a puff sleeve and tie the ends very securely. Trim and push the knot through the gap.

ADDING THE SKIRT

11 Mark the centre top edge of the skirt. Machine stitch a line of long, straight gathering stitches along the top edge, leaving 15mm unstitched at each end. With right sides facing, pin the skirt to the bodice, matching the corners and centres. Pull up one of the threads to gather the skirt so that it fits the bodice. Adjust the gathers so that they lie evenly. Pin, tack and machine stitch together, then zigzag the seam allowance and press it upwards. With right sides facing, pin and tack the side edges together from the sleeve cuff to the hem. Machine stitch, then trim and zigzag the seam allowances. Zigzag both back edges.

12 Join the bottom 8cm of the back edges together with a 1cm seam. Press the seam open, then press back 1cm along either side of the opening. Slip stitch down the turnings. Neaten the bottom edge and make a 15mm hem. Using three strands of pink cotton embroidery thread, make two hand-stitched button loops (see page 121) on the left edge of the bodice and sew the buttons to the right edge in the corresponding positions.

Shoes

CUTTING OUT
from dark grey felt
   two inside uppers
   two outside uppers
from light grey felt
   two soles

MAKING THE SHOES

13 Pin the inside uppers and outside uppers together at the side edges. Oversew together (see page 123). Pin the sole to the bottom edge, matching the centre top and bottom to the seam lines at points A and B. Turn right side out. Sew the end of the strap in place, then stitch on a button. Make up the other shoe in the same way, checking that the strap lies in the opposite direction before you start stitching.

Top & Skirt

CUTTING OUT

from pink cotton fabric
    one top front
    two top backs
from pink print cotton fabric
    one facing
    one 25 x 15cm rectangle, for the skirt

MAKING THE SHIRT

14 Pin and stitch the top backs to the front along the shoulder seams. Trim and zigzag the seams. Zigzag the centre back edges and the outer edge of the facing. With right sides facing, stitch the facing to the neck edge. Trim the seam back to 3mm, turn the facing to the inside and press. Stitch around the neck from the right side, 4mm from the edge.

15 Make a 6mm hem along each cuff, then join the underarm and side seams. Join the centre back with a 1cm hem from the bottom to 8cm from the neck edge. Press the seam open, including the unstitched part of the opening. Sew down the turnings. Turn up a 1cm hem. Make a buttonhole loop (see page 121) on one side of the back neck edge and then sew a button to the right edge in the corresponding position.

MAKING THE SKIRT

16 Zigzag all four edges of the rectangle. Seam the short edges and press open. Make a 1cm hem around the top and bottom edges, leaving a 1cm gap in the top hem. Using a bodkin or small safety pin, thread the elastic through this gap and around the hem. Draw it up so that the waist measures 25cm. Sew the ends of the elastic securely together, trim and push the elastic back inside the hem. Slip stitch the gap closed.

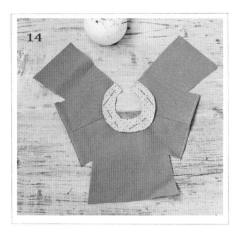

Puppet Show

YOU WILL NEED

for the Puppet theatre
One sheet of A2 mountboard
Selection of coloured pencils or fine
  felt-tip pens
Glue stick or spray mount
Double-sided sticky tape

for the Handpuppets
Basic sewing kit
Glue stick

for the Belle handpuppet
Felt: 20 x 15cm pale pink, 30 x 25cm red,
  15 x 10cm white, 15 x 10 dark brown
10cm red ricrac
Used matchstick
2cm diameter red felt ball or large bead
Cotton embroidery thread in red, brown
  and pale pink

for the Boo handpuppet
Felt: 40 x 30cm dark beige, 15 x 10cm
  white, 10 x 5cm pink, scrap of charcoal
Cotton embroidery thread in pink, white,
  black and dark beige

for the Ava handpuppet
Felt: 20 x 15cm pale pink, 25 x 30cm
  sugar pink, 15cm square dark pink, 15 x
  10cm mustard yellow, scraps of golden
  yellow, black and lilac
Used matchstick
10cm daisy lace
One lace or flower motif
Cotton embroidery thread in yellow, light
  pink and dark pink

for the Cat handpuppet
Felt: 40 x 25cm white, 15 x 10cm
  charcoal, 10 x 10cm pink, 6 x 3cm green
Cotton embroidery thread in grey, pink,
  black and white

Templates: Belle, Boo, Ava and Cat
  Handpuppets on pages 130 and 131.
  The template for the theatre can be
  downloaded from www.quadrille.co.uk/
  belleandboo, which can be printed out
  and coloured in.

SIZE
One size: the theatre is approximately
42 x 35cm and the handpuppets are
approximately 17 x 25cm

PREPARING THE PATTERN PIECES
Enlarge the templates on pages 130–131
by 150%, using a photocopier, and cut out.

CUTTING OUT

BELLE HANDPUPPET
from pale pink felt
  one upper body
from red felt
  one skirt
  ten or twelve 5mm x 5cm strips
from white felt
  one top
from dark brown felt
  one hair
  two eyes

BOO HANDPUPPET
from dark beige felt
  one main body
  two ears, one reversed

from white felt
  one tummy
  one snout
  two eyes
from pink felt
  one nose
  two inner ears, one reversed
  two complete paws
from charcoal felt
  two pupils

AVA HANDPUPPET
from pale pink felt
  one upper body
from sugar pink felt
  one ballgown
from dark pink felt
  two bodices, one reversed
  two overskirts, one reversed
from mustard yellow felt
  one hair
from lilac felt
  one tiara
from golden yellow felt
  two stars
from black felt
  two eyes

CAT HANDPUPPET
from white felt
  one main body
  two ears, one reversed
from charcoal felt
  three patches
  two pupils
  one nose
from pink felt
  two inner ears, one reversed
  two complete paws
from green felt
  two eyes

MAKING THE BELLE HANDPUPPET

1 Using red cotton embroidery thread, stitch Belle's upper body and her skirt together with short running stitches. Decorate the white top with red stripes. Sew the first stripe down the centre with short straight stitches, then fill in on each side. Stitch a length of ricrac along the neckline and tuck the ends to the back. Stitch the striped top in place.

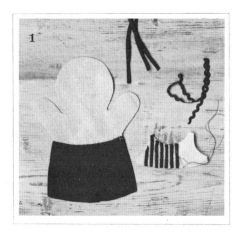

2 Pin on the hair and using short running stitches in brown embroidery thread, sew down the inside edge where it overlaps Belle's face. Add her eyes, then embroider her mouth with two small straight stitches in red embroidery thread for her mouth. Glue the felt ball or bead to the matchstick to make Belle's toffee apple, and then sew it to her hand.

3 Pin the finished front to a sheet of red felt and cut out around the outside edge. Blanket stitch (see page 121) the two together, using pale pink and red embroidery thread to match the felt and leaving the bottom edge open.

MAKING THE CAT HANDPUPPET

4 Pin the three patches in place and sew the inside edges on the cat's body with matching thread. Add the eyes, pupils and nose, and embroider the mouth with three strands of black thread and the whiskers with one strand.

5 Sew the inner ears to the ears around the diagonal edges. Stitch them to the back of the head, overlapping the bottom edges by 1cm. Add the paws. Pin the cat to the remaining white felt and make up as for step 3 of the Belle puppet.

MAKING THE BOO HANDPUPPET

6 Sew Boo's white tummy in place, then add the snout and eyes, checking their positions on the template. Sew the pupils centrally onto the eyes and the nose to the top edge of the snout. Embroider the nose and mouth with three strands of black embroidery thread and the eyelashes and whiskers with a single strand, using straight stitch throughout.

7 Stitch the pink inner ears to the ears. Sew them to the back of the head, overlapping the bottom edges by 1cm. Stitch on the paws – sticking down the individual pieces with a glue stick first makes this easier. Pin Boo to the remaining beige felt and make up as for step 3 of the Belle puppet.

MAKING THE AVA HANDPUPPET

8 Pin the two bodices and two overskirts to the ballgown and stitch them down round the inside edges. Sew the flower motif to the centre, where they meet up. Sew Ava's hair to her body and add her tiara. Stitch on her black eyes and embroider her mouth with pink thread. Sew the body to the back of the gown and trim the neckline with lace. Pin Ava to the remaining sugar pink felt and make up as for step 3 of the Belle puppet.

Cut two tiny stars from the yellow felt. Oversew them together (see page 123), leaving a tiny space at one inner point. Insert the matchstick, securing it with a little glue, then sew the magic wand to Ava's hand.

MAKING THE PUPPET THEATRE

9 Download and print out the theatre proscenium so that the rectangular opening measures 35 x 23cm. Stick the print out onto a sheet of mountboard. Colour in the outline with coloured pencils or fine felt-tip pens, then cut out neatly around the inside and outside edges.

10 From the remaining mountboard, cut two 4 x 45cm strips for the stands. Make two score lines, 16 and 18cm in from the ends. Fold into a triangle and stick the long end to the short, 2cm from the top. Fix one stand to the back of each side column with double-sided tape so that the theatre will stand up.

Treasure Island Map

100 x 70cm heavy unbleached calico
Long ruler or quilter's ruler
Waterproof felt-tip pens in brown, red
  and turquoise
Acrylic craft paints in yellow and
  turquoise
Thick paintbrush
Matching sewing thread
25cm squares of thick felt in pale blue and
  green
25 x 10cm thick brown felt
15 x 10cm each of yellow, orange and
  tangerine felt
12cm square white felt
10cm square of thick red felt
12cm square of fusible bonding web
20 x 13cm blue denim
Bamboo knitting needle
Cotton embroidery thread in dark
  turquoise, orange, white and gold
Brown sewing thread
Two 10 x 12cm rectangles of mid-weight
  brown fabric
Sewing machine
Basic sewing kit

Templates: Treasure island map outline
  and play pieces on pages 132 and 133

SIZE
One size, approximately 95 x 65cm

DRAFTING THE MAP
1 Rule a 92 x 62cm rectangle centrally onto the calico, using a brown pen. Mark a 1cm border around the inside edge, then draw a 10cm grid within that border. You can then draw in your own fantasy map, or follow our guidelines for Boo's Treasure Island on page 133. Starting at the bottom right corner, copy the outline within each little square into the corresponding square on your grid, using a brown pen.

2 Colour in the corner squares on the border with the brown pen, then fill in alternate rectangles with a red pen. Add in the compass, rivers and the volcanoes in brown and the sea routes in turquoise. Give a sandy texture to the beaches with lots of dots and emphasise the rocky terrain with short lines at right angles to the coastline.

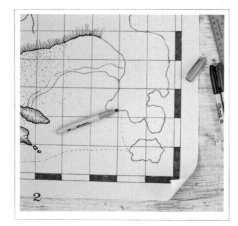

3 Paint in the beaches using a dilute wash of yellow acrylic craft paint. Leave to dry completely, then add the sea using a diluted turquoise acrylic craft paint. Neaten the edges with a double 1cm hem.

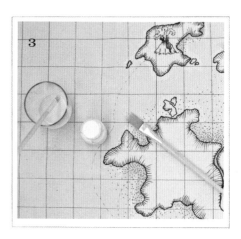

MAKING THE PLAY PIECES
4 Trace the templates for the whale, palm tree, starfish, cross, treasure chest and Jolly Roger flag on pages 132 and 133 and cut them out.

MAKING THE WHALES

5 Pin the whale template onto pale blue felt and cut out around the outside edge. Using dark turquoise cotton embroidery thread, embroider the mouth in back stitch and the eye with a French knot. Make eight whales so that you have a whole school.

MAKING THE PALM TREES

6 Pin the tree-top template onto green felt and the tree-trunk template onto brown felt and cut out around the outside edge. Sew the trunks to the back of the tops with brown cotton sewing thread, reversing the direction of some of them to give a variety of shapes. Make nine palm trees.

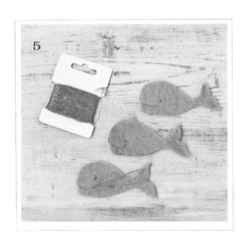

MAKING THE STARFISH

7 Using the star templates, cut out 12 outer stars and 12 inner stars in a mixture of tangerine, orange and yellow felt. Sew the inner stars to the outer stars with rounds of short running stitches in orange cotton embroidery thread, then add a cluster of French knots at the centre of each one.

MAKING THE JOLLY ROGER FLAG

8 Trace the skull and crossbones on page 132 onto the paper side of the fusible bonding web. Cut the shapes out roughly and iron onto white felt, following the manufacturer's instructions. Trim around the outlines, peel off the backing papers and arrange the shapes on the denim rectangle. Press in place. Add a row of small white running stitches around the edges of each shape.

9 Snip a row of raggedy zigzags along the right-hand edge of the flag. Neaten the top and bottom edges with a 6mm hem. Press back a 1cm turning along the left edge and stitch down 5mm from the fold. Smear the pointed end of the bamboo knitting needle with fabric glue; when it is nearly dry, slide it into the channel along the left side.

MAKING THE TREASURE CHEST

10 Pin the lid and lock template onto one of the brown rectangles and draw around the edge with a chalk pencil or air-erasable fabric pen. Fill in the lock with satin stitch (see page 121), using three strands of gold cotton embroidery thread, then work a row of satin stitch along the 'lid'.

11 With right sides facing inwards, pin the two rectangles together and machine stitch, taking a 6mm seam allowance. Clip the corners and turn right side out, then turn under and stitch down a 6mm turning around the opening.

12 Finally, using the template on page 133, cut the cross from red felt and use it to mark the secret location of your hidden treasure.

Ballerina Dress-up

YOU WILL NEED

2m pale pink net, 60cm wide
Strong thread
6cm wide strip of pink cotton fabric, 5cm
    longer than waist measurement
Two large press studs
16 silk flowers with leaves for the tutu
Selection of larger silk flowers, for the
    headdress
Plain headband
Hot glue gun
40 x 160cm pink net, for Boo's tutu
30cm narrow elastic
Safety pin
Matching sewing thread
Sewing machine
Basic sewing kit

SIZE
One size, approximately 25cm long, waist
adjustable to fit

*The pattern pieces and instructions
    for the soft toy Boo on pages 71
    and 72 can be downloaded from
    www.quadrille.co.uk/belleandboo*

GATHERING THE SKIRT
1 Press the net in half lengthways, then
in half again so that you have four layers.
Use a cloth to protect the delicate surface
of the net from the heat of the iron. Using
strong thread, sew a line of gathering
stitches along the top long edge. Pull them
up until the net measures the same length
as the waist measurement. Securely fasten
off the ends.

ADDING THE WAISTBAND
2 Mark a point 15cm down from the top
corners and seam the short edges together
from this point downwards. Trim the
seam. Sew the four layers together on
both sides of the opening.

3 Press under a 1cm seam along one long
and both short edges of the pink cotton
waistband strip. With right sides facing,
pin and tack the raw edge of the strip to
the gathered edge of the skirt so that there
is a 3cm overlap at one end.

4 Machine stitch, then turn the folded
edge to the back, enclosing the net. Pin,
tack and slip stitch down, then sew the
edges of the overlap together. Sew the
pointed parts of the large press studs to
the back of the overlap and the indented
parts to the right side of the waistband.

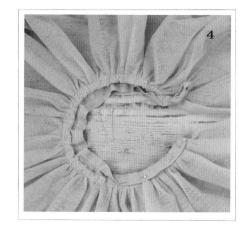

RUCHING THE NET SKIRT

5 Measure all round the skirt hem. Divide this measurement into sixteen and then, using a series of pins, mark sixteen equal sections around the skirt hem.

6 Mark a point 20cm up from each of the pins. Sew a line of gathering stitches between each pair of points and then gather up the net to create the ruched effect. Securely fasten off the thread.

SEWING ON THE FLOWERS

7 Sew a silk flower and a leaf, or leaf spray, to the top point of each line of gathering stitches.

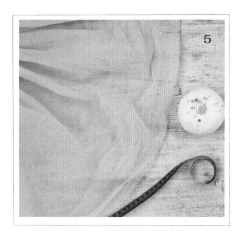

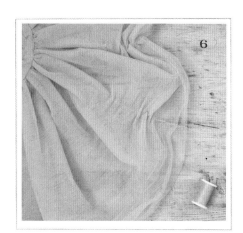

MAKING THE FLORAL HEADDRESS

8 Stick the silk flowers to the hairband, using a hot glue gun. Start at the centre, with the largest blooms, and graduate the sizes so that the smallest lie at the outside edges. Leave the last 8cm at each end of the hairband undecorated.

MAKING BOO'S TUTU

9 Press the strip of pink net in half and then half again lengthways, using a pressing cloth. Sew the short ends together and snip the folds along the bottom edge to separate the layers. Machine stitch around the top edge, 1cm down from the fold, to make a gathering channel.

10 Snip two tiny holes in the wrong side of this gathering channel on either side of the seam. Fix the safety pin to the elastic, thread it through the channel and draw up the ends so that the waist measures 24cm. Sew the ends of the elastic together and trim. Decorate the tutu with any remaining silk flowers.

Felt Forest

Picture frame
Cream paint
Paintbrush
Cream felt to fit the picture frame
PVA adhesive
Fusible bonding web
Sharp pencil
Sharp scissors
Felt in browns, greys, green, white, blue
    and orange

You can also use freezer paper for tracing the templates, which is available from specialist craft shops or quilting suppliers. If you use this method, stick the small details down with a thin layer of PVA.

Templates: Trees, woodland creatures and
    pumpkins on pages 134 and 135

PREPARING THE PICTURE FRAME

1 Paint the picture frame with two or three layers of matte cream paint, leaving it to dry completely between coats. Cover the backing board with matching cream felt, sticking it in place with a thin layer of PVA adhesive. Trim the edges and return the board to the frame.

MAKING THE FELT SHAPES

2 Trace the templates on pages 134 and 135 onto the paper side of the fusible bonding web, using a sharp pencil. Cut each one out roughly, leaving a narrow margin around the shape.

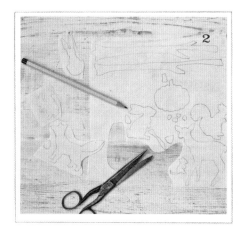

3 Select which colour felt you want to use for each shape. Following the manufacturer's instructions, press the adhesive side of the fusible bonding web onto the coloured felt.

4 Using a pair of sharp scissors, cut out each felt shape, carefully following the pencil outline.

5 Some of the motifs, like the deer and the pumpkin, have extra details in another colour. Follow the main outline for the main shape, then trace and cut out the tiny detail shapes in the same way. Peel off the backing papers and iron the details in place on the larger motifs.

6 Arrange the motifs on the cream felt. You can either leave the felt motifs unfixed to the cream felt backing so your child can create endless imaginary scenes. However, if you want to fix the shapes permanently in place so that you can hang the picture, when you are happy with the layout, peel off the backing papers and iron the felt shapes down.

Tumbling Boo Building Blocks

for each block
18cm square of white cotton or linen
Air-erasable fabric pen or sharp pencil
12cm embroidery hoop
Stranded cotton embroidery thread in
 dark brown, white and light pink
Embroidery needle
Ruler
Five 11cm squares of patterned cotton
 fabric, two each in two different fabrics
 and one in a third fabric
10cm cube of safety-standard foam
Matching sewing thread
Sewing machine
Basic sewing kit

Template: Tumbling Boos (see page 135)

*You can order individually cut foam
 blocks from specialist suppliers, or
 recover old soft toy blocks. Adapt the
 measurement of the squares to fit
 your own foam, allowing a seam
 allowance of 1cm all round.*

SIZE
One size, approximately 9cm square

EMBROIDERING THE BOOS
1 Each of the blocks is embroidered with a different tumbling Boo. Trace one of the motifs on page 135 and cut out around the outside edge. Pin it centrally to the white cotton or linen square. Draw around the outside edge with an air-erasable fabric pen or sharp pencil, then add in the features and other details.

2 Stretch the white cotton or linen square over an embroidery hoop. Stitch over the outlines with a single strand of dark brown cotton embroidery thread. Following the templates, use a mixture of loose back stitch for the straight lines and short angled straight stitches for the tail, broken lines and fine details such as the toes and nose (see pages 120–121), using dark brown cotton embroidery thread.

3 Embroider the whiskers in back stitch and the eyes with satin stitch. Add small white French knots to highlight the eyes and fill in the inner ears with pink satin stitch. Remove the fabric square from the embroidery hoop and press lightly from the wrong side. Trim the fabric square down to 11cm square, keeping the embroidered motif central.

PREPARING THE SQUARES
4 For accurate sewing, it helps to mark the seam lines onto the square. Rule a line 6mm in from each outside edge, using an air-erasable fabric pen or a sharp pencil and a ruler.

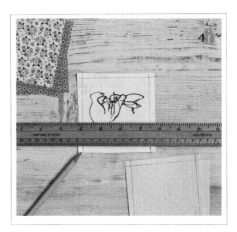

MAKING UP THE BLOCK

5 Lay out the first four squares in a row, alternating the different print fabrics. With right sides facing, pin and machine stitch the first two together. Secure both ends of the seam with reverse stitches and leave the seam allowance at the bottom ends unstitched. Add the other two squares, then join the first square to the fourth square.

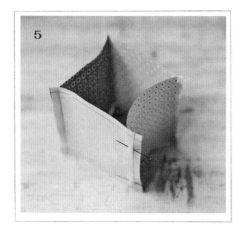

6 Press all the seams open, then press back a 6mm turning around the top (stitched) edge. Turn back and press the seam allowance on each side of the remaining square.

7 Pin the white square embroidered with Boo right side down to the raw edge of the cover, opening out the seams to fit around the corners. Pin, tack and then machine stitch, carefully following the marked seam lines.

8 Clip a small triangle from each corner. Turn right side out and ease out the corners. Tack the seam allowances down so that they lie across the embroidered Boo square: this will ensure that the seam lines don't get twisted when the foam cube is inserted.

FINISHING OFF

9 Fit the fabric cover over the foam cube – it will be a snug fit – and pin the top edge of the cover to the foam. Pin the final fabric square to the top of the cover and slip stitch it in place all round the top edge.

Woodland Masks

for each mask
Fusible bonding web
Sharp pencil
Iron
Sewing machine
Basic sewing kit
Matching sewing thread (optional)
25cm hat elastic

for the Fox mask
Felt in the following colours:
20 x 15cm light grey
20 x 15cm red-brown
10 x 5cm white
3 x 2cm dark brown

for the Deer mask
Felt in the following colours:
25 x 20cm light grey
10 x 10cm white
15 x 10cm light beige
25 x 15cm brown
5 x 3cm dark brown

for the Squirrel mask
Felt in the following colours:
25 x 15cm light grey
10 x 5cm light beige
5 x 5cm white
5 x 3cm dark brown

for the Owl mask
Felt in the following colours:
20 x 15cm light brown
20 x 15cm mid-brown
15 x 10cm cream
3 x 4cm gold

Templates: fox, deer, squirrel and owl on
pages 136 and 137

SIZE
One size, approximately 16–20cm wide
and 14–18cm tall

PREPARING THE PATTERN PIECES
1 Enlarge the templates for the fox, deer,
owl and squirrel masks on pages 135 and
136 by 150%, using a photocopier. Cut
out around the outside edges and the eye
holes. You will use these templates to cut
out the main mask shapes. Trace the other
elements for each animal mask separately
onto the paper side of the fusible bonding
web, leaving a narrow margin around
each shape. Cut them out roughly.

EDGING THE SHAPES
2 The fusible bonding web will hold the
layers of felt together securely, so there is
no need to do any extra sewing. However,
if you would like to add some extra detail,
you can trim the appliqué shapes with
machine stitching, as shown on the fox
mask. Stitch around the outside edge
of each felt piece with a narrow zigzag
or buttonhole-type edging stitch, using
sewing thread in a colour to match the felt.

MAKING THE FOX MASK
3 Using the paper template, cut out the
main mask piece from light grey felt.
Following the manufacturer's instructions
and with the adhesive side downwards,
iron the roughly cut-out fusible bonding
web head shape onto the red-brown felt,
the ear shapes onto the white felt and
the nose shape onto the dark brown felt.
Cut out the felt shapes neatly around
the pencil outlines. Peel off the backing
papers and, using a hot iron, press each
felt piece in position. Edge with matching
sewing thread if preferred.

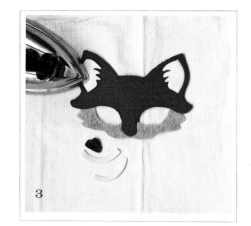

MAKING THE DEER MASK

4 Using the paper template, cut out the main mask piece from light grey felt. Following the manufacturer's instructions and with the adhesive side downwards, iron the roughly cut-out fusible bonding web head shape onto the brown felt. Cut out the felt shape neatly around the pencil outline. Peel off the backing paper and, using a hot iron, press in place.

5 Following the manufacturer's instructions and with the adhesive side downwards, iron the roughly cut-out fusible bonding web spots and eye lash shapes onto the white felt, the ears onto the light beige felt and the nose onto the dark brown felt. Cut out the felt shapes neatly around the pencil outlines. Peel off the backing papers and, using a hot iron, press the ears and spots onto the head, the eyelashes below the eye holes and the nose just overlapping the bottom of the head.

7 Using a hot iron, press the mid-brown felt head shape centrally onto the main mask piece and then add the cream felt round eyes and the gold felt beak.

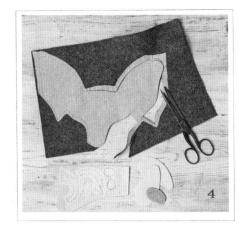

MAKING THE OWL MASK

6 Using the paper template, cut out the main mask piece from light brown felt. Following the manufacturer's instructions and with the adhesive side downwards, iron the roughly cut-out fusible bonding web head shape onto the mid-brown felt, the eyes onto the cream felt and the beak onto the gold felt. Cut out all the felt shapes neatly around the pencil outlines. Peel off the backing papers.

Making the squirrel mask

8 Using the paper template, cut out the main mask piece from light grey felt. Following the manufacturer's instructions and with the adhesive side downwards, iron the roughly cut-out fusible bonding web head shape onto the remaining grey felt, the ears onto the light beige felt, the eye outlines onto the white felt and the nose onto the dark brown felt. Cut out all the felt shapes neatly around the pencil outlines. Peel off the backing papers and, using a hot iron, press each felt piece in place.

Adding the elastic

9 Tie a knot in each end of the elastic. Hand sew securely to the back of the mask, just above the eye holes.

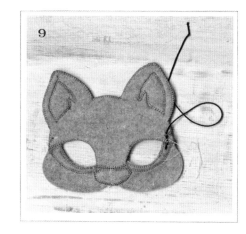

Honey Bear

YOU WILL NEED

100cm x 50cm golden brown bouclé wool
   or faux fur
Two black safety toy eyes or buttons,
   1cm in diameter
Safety-standard polyester toy filling
Toy filling beads
20cm x 10cm light or golden brown
   velvet, for paw pads
Five three-part safety plastic toy joints,
   4cm in diameter
Cotton embroidery thread in black
Matching sewing thread
Sewing machine
Basic sewing kit

Templates: Honey Bear (see pages 138
   and 139)

SIZE
One size: approximately 40cm tall

PREPARING THE PATTERN PIECES
Enlarge the templates for the bear on pages
138 and 139 by 150%, using a photocopier.

CUTTING OUT
from bouclé wool or faux fur
   two side heads, one reversed
   one head gusset
   four ears
   two outer arms, one reversed
   two inner arms, one reversed
   two outer legs, one reversed
   two inner legs, one reversed
   two bodies, one reversed
   one tail
from velvet
   two front paw pads, one reversed
   two back paw pads, one reversed

Mark and then pierce the positions for the
two safety eyes on the two sides heads,
along with the positions for the four
washers on both bodies, the inner arms
and the inner legs.

SEAMS
As you sew together the Honey Bear,
reinforce the ends of every seam with
reverse stitches to strengthen the joins.

The seam allowance throughout is 1cm,
but for the darts it is 6mm.

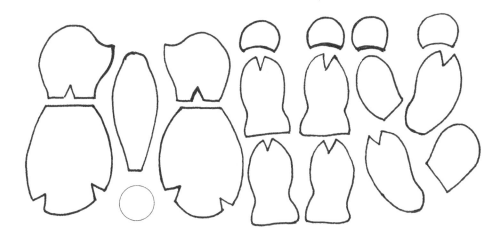

CUTTING GUIDE

MAKING HONEY BEAR'S HEAD

1 With right sides together, pin and tack the small dart at the neck edge of each of the two side heads, matching points A. Machine stitch the darts. Pin one of the side heads to the head gusset from points B to C (from the nose to the back neck edge). Pin and tack together, then machine stitch the seam. Join the other side head in two stages, from points B to D (from the nose to the front neck edge) and then from points D to E (from the nose to the back neck edge).

2 Trim the seam allowances back to 6mm and turn the head right side out. If you are using safety eyes, fix them to both the side heads. Fill the head firmly with safety-standard toy filling. Using a double length of strong thread, stitch a round of small running stitches around the neck edge. Place one of the pegged discs from a toy joint inside the gap, so that the peg faces outwards. Draw up the thread and securely fasten.

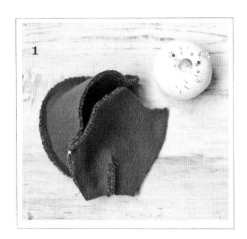

ATTACHING HONEY BEAR'S EARS

3 Pin and tack the ears together in pairs from points F to F. Machine stitch the seams, leaving the straight bottom edge open, and trim the seam allowances back to 6mm. Turn the ears right side out. Turn under the 1cm allowance along the bottom edge of the ears and tack the sides together along the opening. Following the line indicating the position of the ears on the template, pin the ears to the head and then sew them securely in place.

SEWING HONEY BEAR'S BODY

4 With right sides together, pin and tack the small darts at the tummy and bottom, matching points G at the front and points H at the back. Machine stitch the darts. With right sides together, pin the two bodies together. Machine stitch the seam from point I (the front neck edge) round to point J (the lower back). Leave a small opening for adding the safety-standard toy filling. Make a short seam from point K to the back neck edge. Tack down the seam allowance on either side of the opening. Turn right side out.

5 Using a double length of strong thread, stitch a round of small running stitches 5mm below the neck edge.

6 Leaving a tiny gap at the centre, draw up the thread and securely fasten. Pour the toy beads into the body cavity, filling it until it is approximately one third full. Then fill the rest of the body with safety-standard toy filling.

ASSEMBLING HONEY BEAR'S ARMS

7 Pin and tack the small darts at the shoulder of the outer arms, matching points J. Machine stitch the darts. Sew the velvet front paw pads to the ends of the inner arms, taking a 6mm seam allowance. Pin and tack the inner and outer arms together, easing the curves so that they fit neatly around the shoulder. Machine stitch, leaving a gap at the back of the arms between the two points marked K.

8 Turn under the 1cm allowance on either side of the opening and tack. Trim the rest of the seam allowance back to 6mm. Turn the arm right side out. Firmly stuff the lower part of the arm. Push the pegged disc from a toy joint through the hole in the inner arm. Finish stuffing the arm, then slip stitch the opening to close (see page 123). Make up the second arm in the same way.

ASSEMBLING HONEY BEAR'S LEGS

9 Pin and tack the small darts at the thighs of the outer legs, matching points L. Machine stitch the darts. With right sides together, pin and tack the inner and outer legs together. Machine stitch from points M to N (from the toe to the heel), leaving an opening between the two points marked L. Pin the velvet back paw pads to the foot openings, matching points M and N and easing the two fabrics together around the curves. Tack with small stitches and then machine stitch, taking a 1cm seam allowance. Turn under the 1cm allowance on either side of the opening and tack. Trim the other seam allowance back to 6mm.

10 Turn the leg right side out. Firmly stuff the lower part of the leg. Push the pegged disc from a toy joint through the hole in the inner leg. Finish stuffing the leg, then slip stitch the opening to close. Make up the second leg in the same way.

Sewing Honey Bear together

11 Push the left arm through the left armhole. Fix on the washer and the locking disc from inside the body and squeeze the three pieces tightly together until they click into place. If the locking discs are proving tricky to fix, try softening the plastic first by soaking the toy joints in very hot water for a few minutes. Add the other limbs and the head in the same way.

12 Using all six strands of the black stranded cotton embroidery thread, embroider the nose with long satin stitches (see page 121). If using buttons for eyes, securely sew them in place.

Adding Honey Bear's tail

13 Sew a round of long gathering stitches all the way round the circumference of the tail piece. Pull up the gathering stitches slightly, fill the space with a small amount of safety-standard toy filling and then pull the stitches more tightly to close. Oversew (see page 123) the tail to Honey Bear's bottom.

Bedtime With Bear

for the sleeping bag and pyjama case
Quilter's ruler and air-erasable fabric pen
  or chalk pencil
Matching sewing thread
Sewing machine
Basic sewing kit

for Honey Bear's sleeping bag
50 x 110cm patterned cotton fabric, for
  the outer sleeping bag and binding
50 x 85cm checked or plain cotton fabric,
  for the lining
50 x 85cm cotton quilt wadding
Safety-standard polyester toy filling

for the pyjama case
32 x 84cm patterned cotton fabric, for the
  outer case and binding
32 x 64cm checked or plain cotton fabric,
  for the lining
32 x 64cm cotton quilt wadding

Honey Bear's Sleeping Bag

SIZE
One size, approximately 45 x 50cm

CUTTING OUT
from patterned cotton fabric
> one 45 x 35cm rectangle for the
> quilted front
> one 45 x 50cm rectangle for the back
> two 4 x 50cm binding strips
> two 4 x 55cm binding strips

from plain cotton fabric
> one 45 x 35cm rectangle for lining
> the front
> one 45 x 50cm rectangle for lining
> the back

from cotton quilt wadding
> one 45 x 35cm rectangle for the front
> one 45 x 50cm rectangle for the back

PREPARING THE FRONT
1 Lay out the front lining fabric with the
right side facing downwards, with the
front quilt wadding on top and the front
patterned fabric right side up on top. Quilt
these layers together in a diamond pattern,
as given in steps 1 to 2 of the Pyjama
Case. Bind the top edge of the quilted
front with one of the short binding strips,
as given in step 3 of the Pyjama Case.

MAKING UP THE BACK
2 Lay out the back patterned fabric with
the right side facing downwards, with the
back quilt wadding on top and the back
lining fabric right side up on top of the
wadding. Mark a line 20cm down from
the top edge and stitch along it to make
the division for the pillow section.

JOINING THE FRONT AND BACK
3 Pin and tack the front and back pieces
together along the bottom edges, then
bind this edge with a short binding strip.

FINISHING OFF THE SLEEPING BAG
4 Neaten the two long side edges with the long binding strips. Lightly stuff the pillow section with safety-standard toy filling, slipping it between the back fabric and the back quilt wadding. Tack the top edges together and bind with the remaining binding strip.

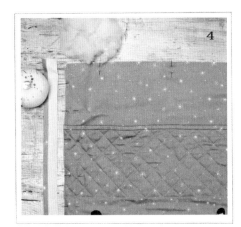

Pyjama Case

SIZE
One size, approximately 32 x 25cm

CUTTING OUT
from patterned fabric

    one 32 x 64cm rectangle for the bag
If your fabric is directional, like ours, make sure that the part you wish to appear on the front of the bag lies at the top of the rectangle. You may need to join two pieces so that any border design lies in the right place.
    two 4 x 35cm binding strips
    two 4 x 44cm binding strips

MARKING THE QUILT LINES
1 Using the quilter's ruler and an air-erasable fabric pen or chalk pencil, rule a series of parallel lines, 2.5cm apart, across the main fabric. Rule a second set of lines at right angles, so that the whole surface is covered with a diamond grid. Leave any border patterns, like this bedtime parade, unstitched: draw a line above and below the design and stitch along them both.

QUILTING THE FABRIC
2 Lay out the lining fabric with the right side facing downwards, then place the quilt wadding on top. Position the main fabric right side up on top, lining up the corners. Insert rows of pins between the lines, in one direction only. Using a thread to match the fabric, stitch along the set of marked lines that lie between the pins. Remove the pins, then sew along the other lines. Trim the edges of the quilted fabric.

BINDING THE SHORT EDGES

3 Press under a 1cm turning along one long edge of each binding strip. With right sides facing, pin one short strip to the right side of one short edge of the pyjama case. Machine stitch 1cm from the edge, then turn the folded edge to the back. Pin down and slip stitch the folded edge to the lining. Trim the ends. Bind the other short edge in the same way.

MAKING UP THE PYJAMA CASE

4 Lay the pyjama case out with the lining facing upwards and turn up the bottom 25cm to make the pocket. Pin and then tack the sides edges together. Bind the side edges with the remaining binding strips, neatening the ends by tucking under a 1cm fold at each corner.

Hobby Horse

60 x 35cm mid-weight fabric
Safety-standard polyester toy stuffing
20 x 15cm black suede or felt
Two 2cm diameter black buttons
Long needle
110cm black cotton tape, 12mm wide
Four 15mm metal rings
100g chunky brown wool yarn
20 x 10cm corrugated cardboard
Hot glue gun
2cm diameter pole, 80cm long
Red spotted neckerchief
Strong sewing thread
Sewing machine
Basic sewing kit

Templates: Hobby horse head, ear and
nostrils (see page 140)

SIZE
One size, approximately 110cm

PREPARING THE PATTERN PIECES
Enlarge the templates on page 140 by
150%, using a photocopies, and cut out.

CUTTING OUT
from mid-weight fabric
two heads, one reversed
two ears, one reversed
from suede or felt
two ears, one reversed
two nostrils

MARKING UP
1 Mark the eye and ear positions on both
sides of the head pieces.

STITCHING THE HEAD DARTS
2 With the right side of the fabric facing
inwards, fold the nose on head piece so
that the two points A match up. Pin the
two sides together, then machine stitch the
dart, taking a 6mm seam allowance. Do
the same on the other head piece.

SEWING UP THE HEAD
3 Pin and tack the two heads together
with right sides facing and darts matching.
Machine stitch, taking a 6mm seam
allowance, leaving the bottom edge open.
Turn right side out and stuff the head and
the top part of the neck firmly with safety-
standard toy filling.

ADDING THE EYES & NOSE
4 Stitch a nostril to each side of the
head, positioning them over the ends of
the darts. Sew the two buttons onto the
marked points with a double length of
strong thread and a long needle. Give
shape to the head by pushing the needle
right through the snout and through both
buttons, then pulling up the thread before
securely fastening off.

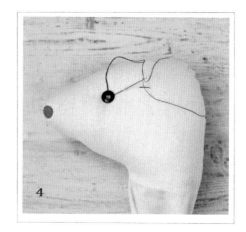

... AND THE EARS

5 Pin the fabric and felt or suede ears together in pairs, again with right sides facing. Machine stitch 6mm from the edge, leaving the bottom edge open. Trim the seam allowance back to 3mm, then turn right side out and lightly press. Fold in half, with the main fabric on the outside, and stitch along the bottom edge.

6 Make two small cuts in the head, snipping along the marked ear positions. Tuck the ears into the slits, and stitch securely in place.

MAKING THE HARNESS

7 For the noseband, cut two 15cm lengths of tape. Join a metal ring to each end of the first length, turning back and stitching down a 1cm turning. Add the other piece of tape to make a loop. Cut a 25cm length of tape for the browband. Join this to a 20cm length, using the other two rings, to make a larger loop.

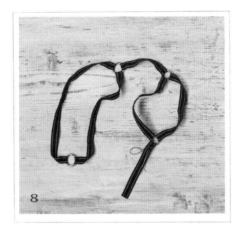

8 Join the two loops with two 10cm lengths of tape for the cheek pieces. Fit the harness on the hobby horse's head. Cut a final length of tape for the headpiece that goes around the back of the head and sew the ends to the browband loops.

ADDING THE MANE

9 Cut the yarn into 24cm long strands. The easiest way to do this is to wind it around a 12cm wide strip of card, then snip through the centre. Take four or five strands at a time, fold them in half and then back stitch them securely along the head seam. Start stitching just behind the headband and finish 5cm from the bottom opening.

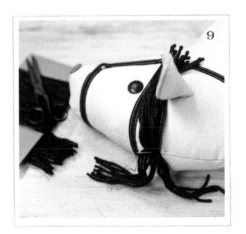

ATTACHING THE POLE

10 From thick corrugated cardboard, cut two 9cm discs and snip out a 2cm circle from the centre of each. Stick them together with a hot glue gun, then slide the double disc over the pole so that it lies 12cm down from the top end.

11 Using a double strand of the strong sewing thread, sew a round of running stitches around the neck edge. Push the top of the pole into the neck, adding more stuffing if necessary, then partly draw up the thread. Add more stuffing below the disc, then draw up and secure the thread. Finish off by folding the neckerchief in half diagonally and tying it around the neck.

Christmas Ornaments

Templates: Boo template on page 141

YOU WILL NEED

for the salt dough
2 cups self-raising flour
1 cup table salt
1 cup water
Mixing bowl
Wooden spoon
Pastry board
Rolling pin
Baking tray
Baking parchment
Kitchen knife
Spatula
Toothpick or bamboo skewer
Selection of holly leaf, heart and star
  biscuit cutters
Selection of twine or ribbon for hanging

MAKING THE SALT DOUGH

1 Place the self-raising flour and table salt in a large bowl. Make a well in the centre and pour in the water. Stir together thoroughly, until you have a doughy consistency. Add more water if it seems too dry and add more flour if it is sticky.

2 Knead the ball of dough on a floured surface for two minutes, then leave to rest for 30 minutes in the fridge. Roll the dough out evenly to a thickness of about 1cm. Line a baking tray with baking parchment.

CUTTING OUT THE BOO SHAPES

3 Place the Boo template on the surface of the dough and cut out around the edge with a kitchen knife. Gently lift the shape onto a spatula and place it on the baking parchment. Smooth the edges with a damp finger.

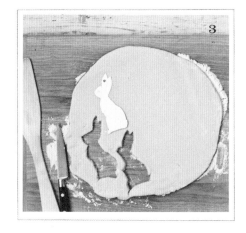

4 Add the line details with a toothpick or skewer and twiddle the point into the dough to make Boo's eye. Push it right through the ear to make the hanging hole, easing the dough back into shape if it distorts too much.

MODELLING A HOLLY LEAF

5 Cut out the holly leaf in the same way, smooth the edges and mark the veins. Make a hanging hole at the top. The three berries are made by rolling out tiny balls of dough. Dab the backs with water and gently press them in place. Mark the dots with the skewer.

EMBELLISHING A STAR

8 Once you start to look around, you'll find lots of little items that can be used to make interesting patterns on your salt dough. Buttons, cutlery, and even dressmaking pins can be pressed into the surface to create new texture.

BAKING THE ORNAMENTS

9 Set your oven to the lowest setting and leave the biscuits to bake slowly for four hours. Take out and allow to cool, then thread them onto twine or ribbon and knot the ends to hang.

5

8

DECORATING A HEART

6 Use a large heart biscuit cutter to make the basic shape and leave the cutter in place (this prevents the heart from distorting as you add the extra details). Roll some of the dough so that it is thinner and cut out a few small hearts and stars. Fix them onto the heart with a dab of water. Add extra texture to the background by making indentations with a pencil point. Make a hanging hole at the centre top, then transfer the heart to the baking tray.

Advent Calendar

120 x 70cm cream canvas
Sharp pencil or air-erasable fabric pen
Ruler
135 x 30cm printed cotton fabric
230cm bias binding, 12mm wide
Stranded cotton embroidery thread in red
60cm tape, 2cm wide
60cm square of denim or mid-weight
  fabric, for the back panel
80cm length of dowelling or bamboo
1m string
Matching sewing thread
Sewing machine
Basic sewing kit

Templates: Numbers 1 through to 0 on
  page 141

SIZE
57cm square, plus hanging loops

CUTTING OUT
from cream canvas
  one 60cm square for main panel
  four 50 x 9cm rectangles for the
  pocket strips
from printed cotton fabric
  12 rectangles, 10cm wide and 8cm
  high, each with a motif at the centre

PREPARING THE POCKET STRIPS
1 Press under a 1cm turning at the short
ends of each pocket strip. Using a sharp
pencil or air-erasable fabric pen and
a ruler, draw five vertical lines at 8cm
intervals along the fabric strips to mark
the six individual pockets.

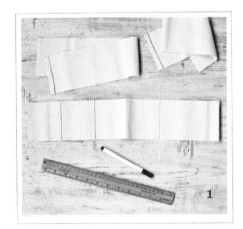

ADDING THE MOTIFS
2 Press under a 1cm turning along both
side edges of the twelve motif rectangles.
Pin the motifs to the second, fourth and
sixth divisions on two of the strips and to
the first, third and fifth divisions on the
other two. Match up the edges with the
marked lines, then machine stitch them
in place, close to the fold.

FINISHING THE TOP EDGES
3 Bind the top edge of each strip with
a 52cm length of bias binding (see page
122). Tuck the overlap in at each end to
neaten the top corners.

EMBROIDERING THE NUMBERS

5 Trace or photocopy the number templates on page 141 and cut them out. Start by pinning the '1' centrally to the first space of the first strip, 2.5cm up from the lower edge. Draw around it with a fabric marker or pencil and embroider over the line with running stitch, using four strands of red thread. Continue stitching numbers in alternate spaces, omitting those that would appear on the pockets with motifs, until you reach '24'.

ATTACHING THE POCKETS

6 Draw a 45cm line across the main panel, 14cm down from the top edge. Now rule three more lines at 13cm intervals. With the right side facing downwards, pin and tack the raw edge of the first pocket strip centrally along the top line.

7 Machine the pocket strip in place, then fold it upwards and press the seam. Insert a pin at each end, then in the centre of each pocket. Machine stitch the pocket divisions, starting each line below the binding and reinforcing both ends of each line. Add the other three strips in the same way.

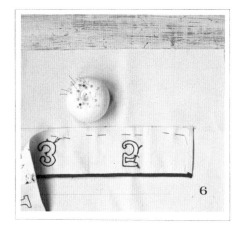

PUTTING IT TOGETHER

8 Cut the tape into four 15cm lengths and fold them in half to make the hanging loops. With raw edges matching, and right sides facing, pin one loop to each top corner of the backing panel. Mark two points, 14cm in from the inside edges of the tapes, and pin the other two loops to these points. Tack all four loops securely in place.

9 With right sides facing, pin and tack the back and front together around the side and top edges, double checking that both pieces are the right way up. Machine stitch, taking a 15mm seam allowance.

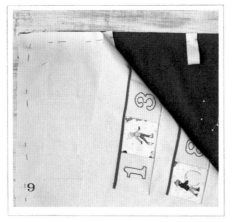

10 Clip a small triangle from each top corner, cutting to within 3mm of the seam line; this reduces the bulky seam allowance, giving you sharp corners. Turn right side out, ease out the corners and press the seams lightly from the back. Press under a 15mm turning around the bottom opening, then pin and tack the front and back together and machine stitch 3mm from the edge.

11 Insert the length of dowelling or bamboo through the loops, tie one end of the string to each end and hang the calendar from a picture or coat hook.

Techniques

All of the basic techniques that you'll need to make the Belle & Boo sewing projects, from Ava's Play Tent (page 12) to the Tumbling Boo Building Blocks (page 80) are illustrated here: including seaming, hemming, binding and simple embroidery stitches. You'll find anything else that you need to know will be explained in the step-by-step project instructions.

Embroidery

TRANSFERRING OUTLINES

There are several ways to transfer a template onto fabric, but this is the most straightforward. Photocopy or trace the image onto dressmaker's paper and cut out. Draw around the outside edge with a sharp pencil or an air-erasable pen – this gives a line that will disappear over time. Add in the details, referring back to the original template.

MOUNTING IN A HOOP

Mounting the fabric taut within an embroidery hoop will help to keep all of your embroidery stitches neat and regular. Unscrew the two halves of the frame and place the fabric over the inside ring. Place the other ring on top and push it down. Pull the fabric evenly all the way around to increase the tension. Tighten the screw to hold the fabric in place.

STRAIGHT STITCH

This is the simplest embroidery stitch. Single straight stitches are used for details and broken outlines, while straight stitches that are placed close together can be used to quickly fill areas with solid blocks of colour. These stitches can be made at any length and in any direction. Vary the length of the stitches to give more texture.

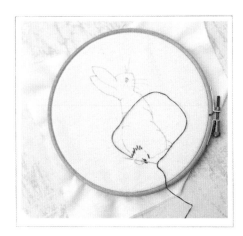

STEM STITCH

This is good for when making outlines: make all the stitches regular for a smooth line, or uneven for a softer, hand-drawn feel. Make a straight stitch from left to right, and then come back up directly alongside and halfway down the previous stitch to make the next. Repeat to the end.

BACK STITCH

This stitch gives a neat line. Work from right to left. Start with a small backwards stitch from left to right, then bring the needle up at the left, leaving a space equal to the first stitch. Take the thread back to the end of the previous stitch. Repeat.

SATIN STITCH

Satin stitch is made up of rows of single vertical straight stitches, worked tightly alongside each other to give a smooth, satiny surface. Create a more random look by working the second row of encroaching satin stitch so that it overlaps the first and angle the stitches to fit within the outline.

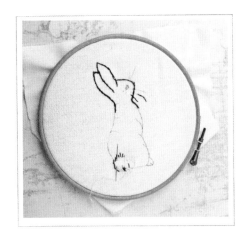

BLANKET STITCH

This is a useful stitch for defining edges and joining layers. Always leave a space between stitches. Push the needle halfway into the fabric and place the length of thread under the needle tip. Draw tight to create a loop at the edge and repeat.

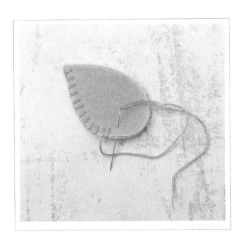

BUTTON LOOP

This old-fashioned fastening loop is perfect for the tiny buttons on the Rag Doll's Summer Dress (pages 50–51). It is similar to blanket stitch but has an extra twist which gives it a firmer edge. Using three strands of cotton embroidery thread, make four fairly loose straight stitches as the foundation bar. Hold the needle under the bar and loop the thread behind it from left to right. Pull the needle through over the thread and gently pull the thread up and back to make a small 'purl' on the outside edge. Practice on spare fabric first and you'll find that this is much easier to do than it is to describe!

Hems

SINGLE HEM

With the wrong side of the fabric facing you, turn up the bottom edge (and the sides, if required) to the depth given in the steps. Use a tape measure to check the hem is the same length all the way along, then tack, pin or press as directed. Stitch in place by hand or machine, 3–4mm from the raw edge.

DOUBLE HEM

Make and press a single turning, as for a single hem, then fold back a second turning to the depth given. Make sure it is the same all the way along and machine stitch 3–4mm from the inside fold. Finish off the bottom edge of the Painter's Smock (page 38) in this way, so that it looks neat from both sides.

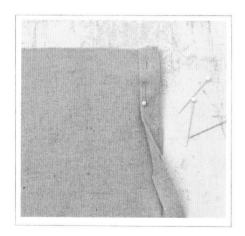

BIAS BINDING

Thicker fabrics, which are too bulky to fold, can be finished with ready-made bias binding. There are two methods of doing this: slotted-over binding, which is quicker to do but leaves very visible stitching lines, and turned binding, which will give a stitch-free look.

1 For the first method, simply fold the binding strip in half lengthways with the raw edges on the inside and slip it over the raw edge. Tack through all the layers and stitch in place 2–3mm from the edge.

2 For the second method, open out one fold of the binding and with right sides facing, pin the raw edge along the edge of the fabric. Machine stitch along the fold. Turn the binding to the other side and tack down the fold, making sure that it lies over and covers the seam line. Sew down from the right side, stitching 'in the ditch': directly over the join between the binding and the fabric. This method is used for binding the doorway edges of Ava's Play Tent (page 12).

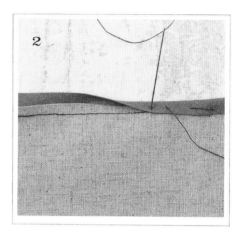

Seams

SINGLE SEAM

1 Pin the two fabric edges that are to be joined together, with the right sides facing. Machine stitch parallel to the edges, using the side of the presser foot or the lines on the sewing machine bed to keep the seam allowance even.

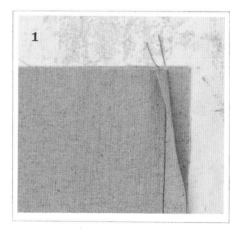

2 'Press open' by parting the two seams with the tip of the iron and press flat.

Hand Stitching

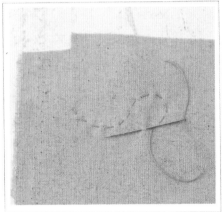

RUNNING STITCH
Large, evenly spaced running stitches can be used for tacking two pieces of fabric together as a temporary join. Smaller running stitches are used for embroidered details, or can be pulled up as a gathering stitch. The spaces between each stitch should be the same length as the stitches themselves.

CORNER SEAM
Sew along the first edge as far as the end of the seam allowance. Keeping the needle down, lift the foot and turn the fabric by ninety degrees. Lower the foot and continue along the second edge. Clip a small triangle of fabric from the corners of the seam allowance to make sure that the seam will lie flat when it is turned right side out, clipping about 3mm away from the stitch line.

OVERSEW
Join two folded edges or thick fabric like the bouclé wool used for Honey Bear (page 92) with this stitch. Tack or hold the two pieces together, with right sides facing, and sew at a right angle through both layers, close to the edge. Make another stitch in exactly the same way, and carry on to the end of the join.

SLIP STITCH
This stitch gives an almost invisible join when stitching together two pieces of fabric. The idea is that most of the stitch is hidden. Bring the needle up 1mm from the edge of the lower piece of fabric. Insert it directly above in the other fabric and come out again 5mm along, at the same level. Make a small downwards stitch into the lower fabric and continue to the end of the seam.

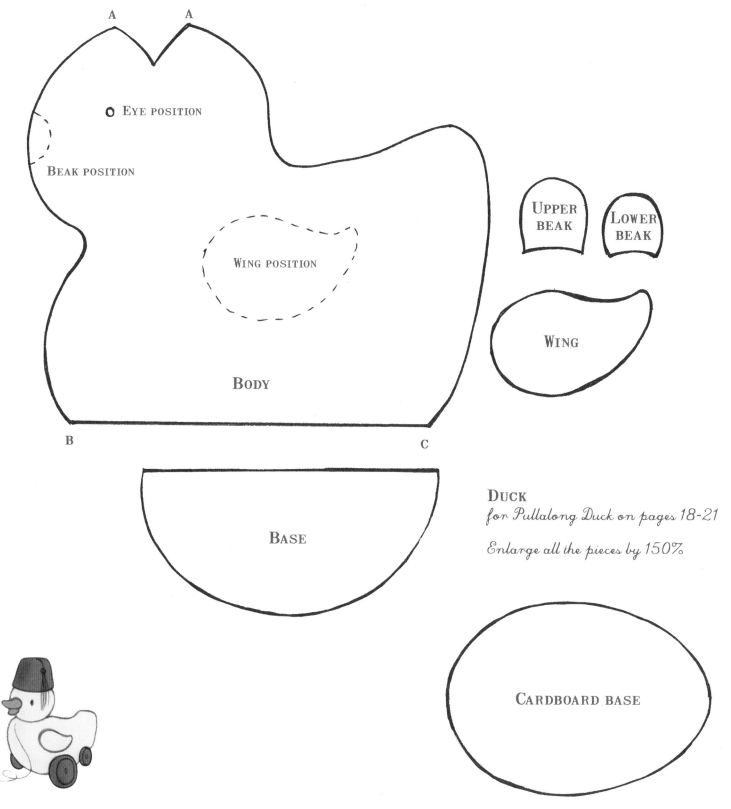

A A

O EYE POSITION

BEAK POSITION

WING POSITION

BODY

B C

UPPER BEAK

LOWER BEAK

WING

BASE

DUCK
for Pullalong Duck on pages 18-21

Enlarge all the pieces by 150%

CARDBOARD BASE

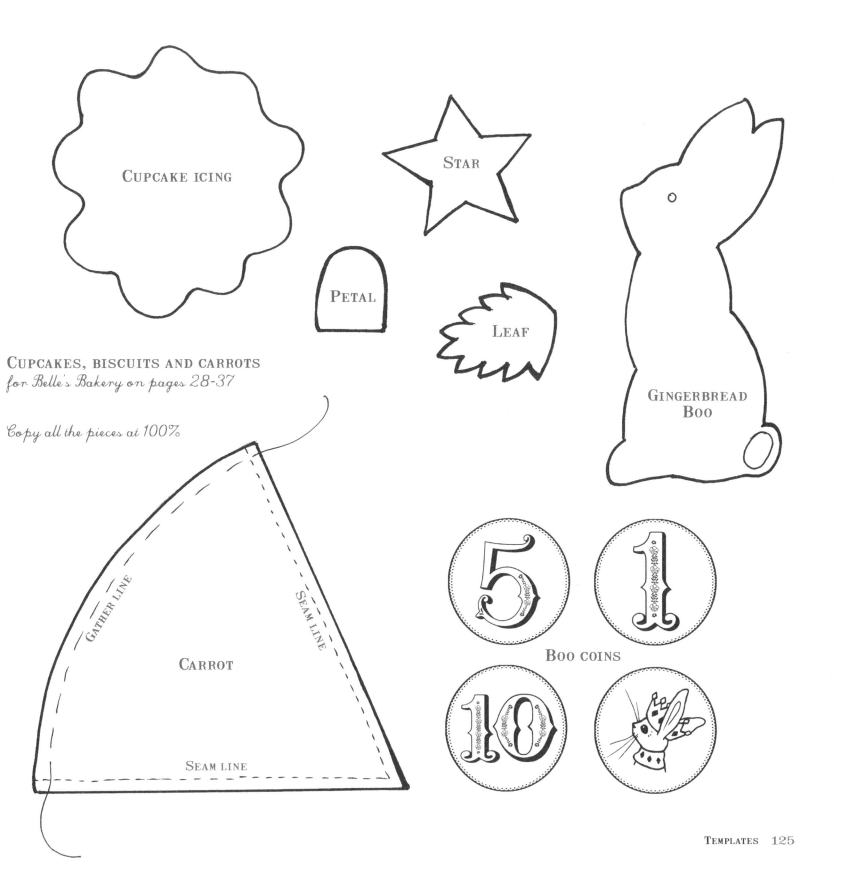

CUPCAKE ICING

STAR

PETAL

LEAF

GINGERBREAD BOO

CUPCAKES, BISCUITS AND CARROTS
for Belle's Bakery on pages 28-37

Copy all the pieces at 100%

GATHER LINE

SEAM LINE

CARROT

SEAM LINE

BOO COINS

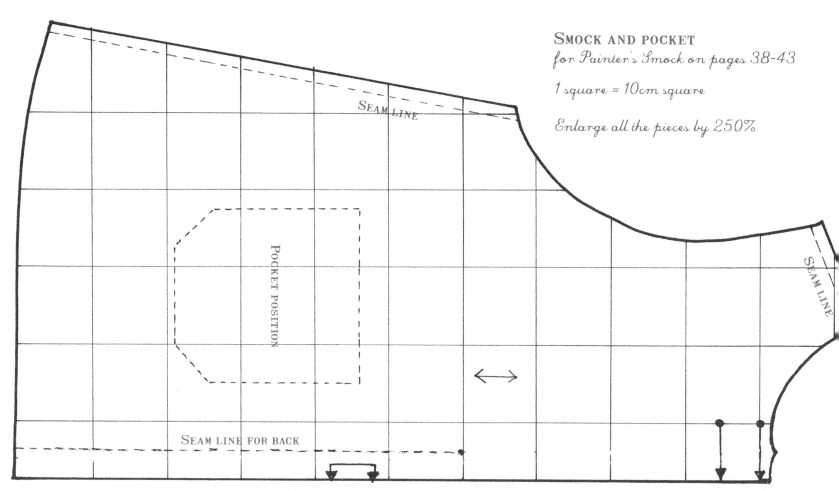

SEAM LINE

POCKET POSITION

SEAM LINE

SEAM LINE FOR BACK

FOLD LINE FOR FRONT

SMOCK AND POCKET
for Painter's Smock on pages 38-43

1 square = 10cm square

Enlarge all the pieces by 250%

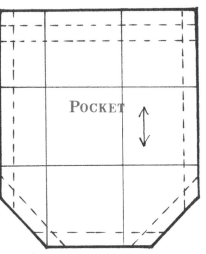

POCKET

126 TEMPLATES

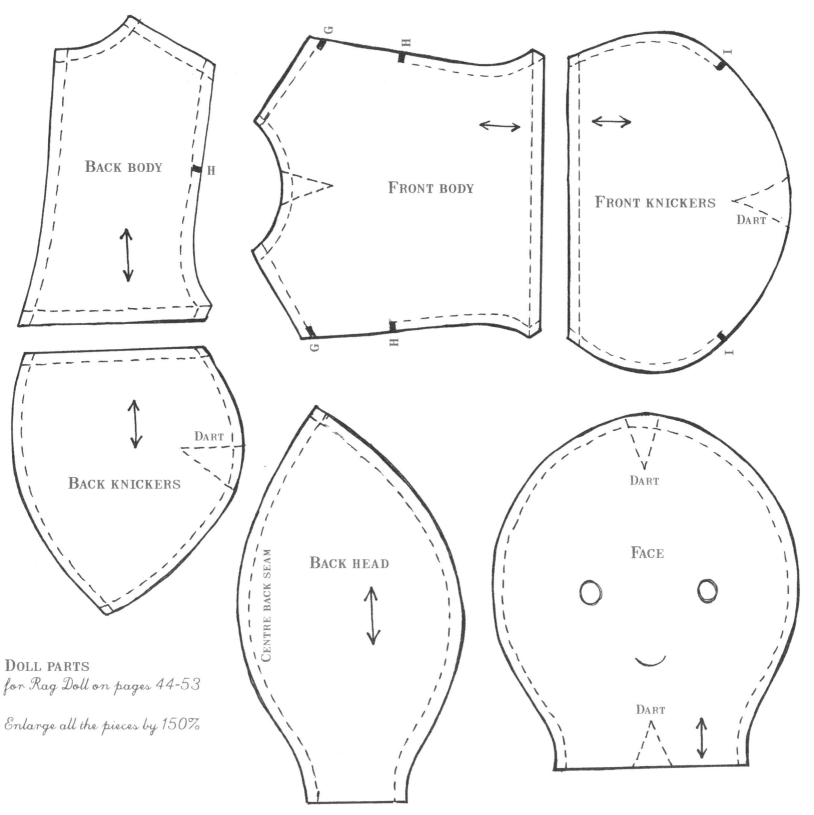

BACK BODY

H

FRONT BODY

G

H

G

H

FRONT KNICKERS

DART

I

I

BACK KNICKERS

DART

BACK HEAD

CENTRE BACK SEAM

FACE

DART

DART

DOLL PARTS
for Rag Doll on pages 44-53

Enlarge all the pieces by 150%

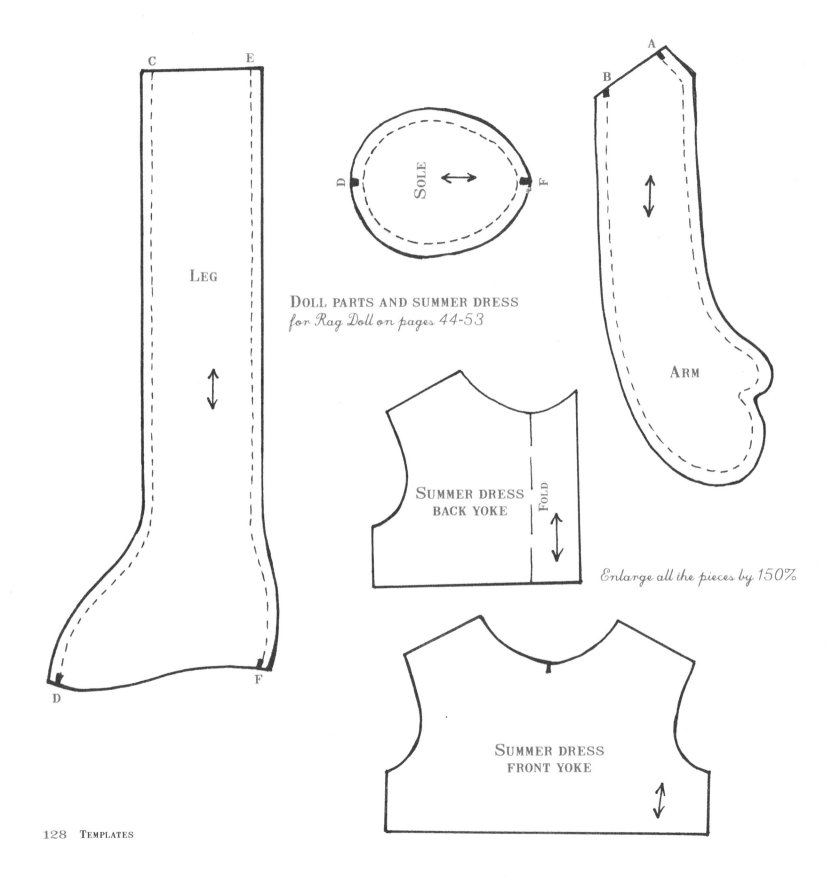

C   E

A

B

SOLE

D   F

LEG

DOLL PARTS AND SUMMER DRESS
for Rag Doll on pages 44-53

ARM

SUMMER DRESS
BACK YOKE

FOLD

Enlarge all the pieces by 150%

F

D

SUMMER DRESS
FRONT YOKE

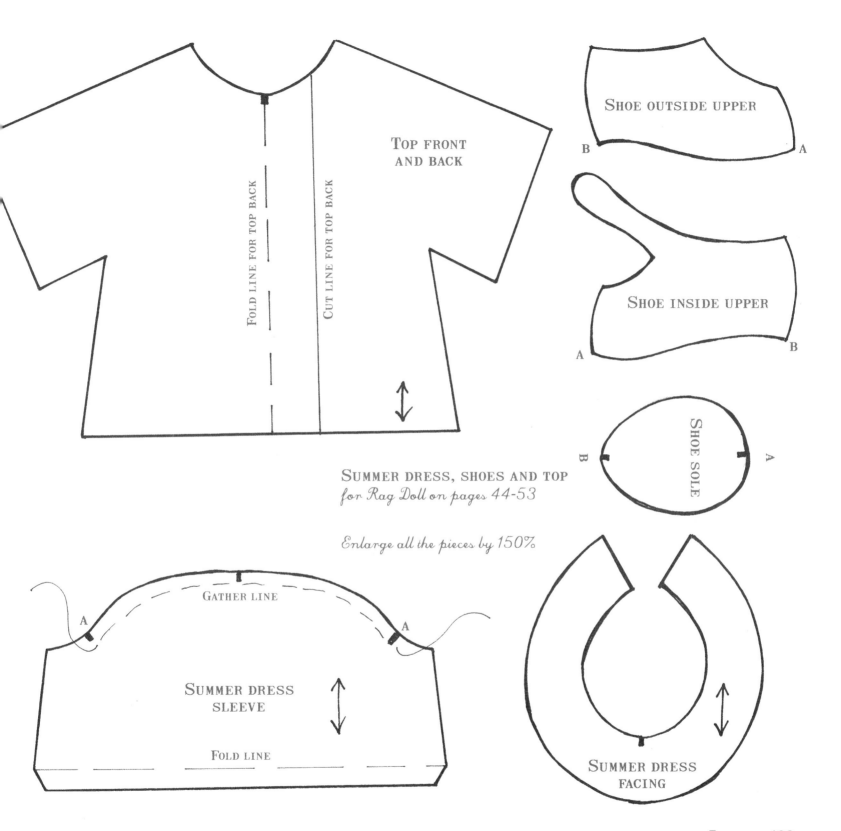

SHOE OUTSIDE UPPER

B   A

SHOE INSIDE UPPER

A   B

TOP FRONT
AND BACK

FOLD LINE FOR TOP BACK

CUT LINE FOR TOP BACK

B   SHOE SOLE   A

SUMMER DRESS, SHOES AND TOP
for Rag Doll on pages 44-53

Enlarge all the pieces by 150%

GATHER LINE

A   A

SUMMER DRESS
SLEEVE

FOLD LINE

SUMMER DRESS
FACING

BELLE

Enlarge all the pieces by 150%

BOO

Ava handpuppet and Cat handpupppet
for Puppet Show pages 54-61

Enlarge all the pieces by 150%

AVA

CAT

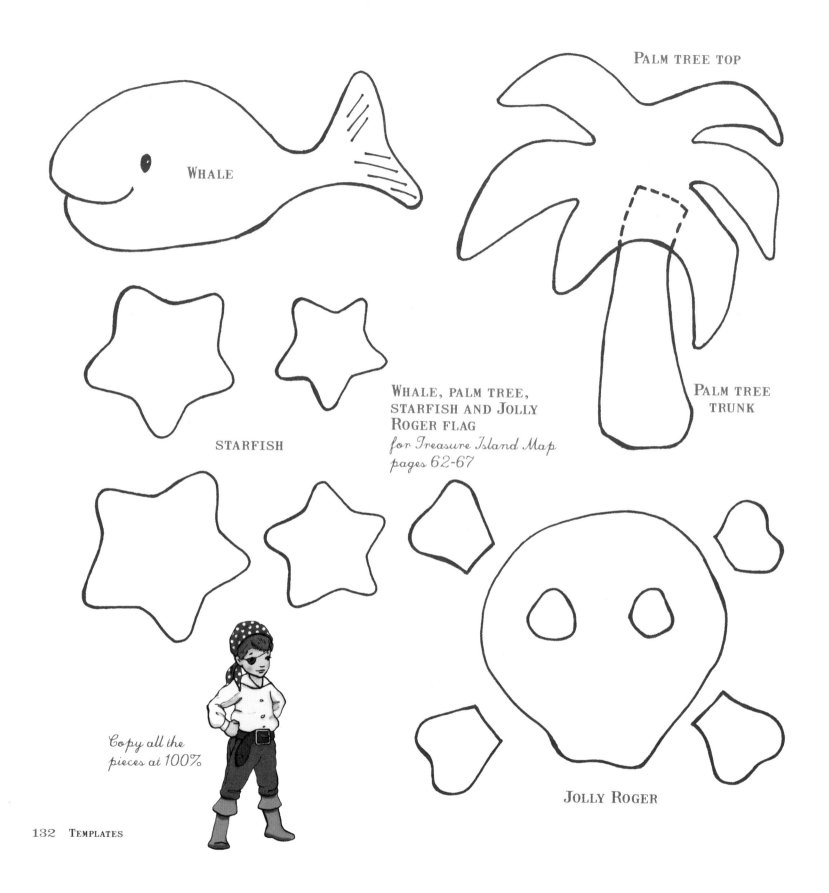

WHALE

PALM TREE TOP

STARFISH

WHALE, PALM TREE, STARFISH AND JOLLY ROGER FLAG

for Treasure Island Map pages 62-67

PALM TREE TRUNK

Copy all the pieces at 100%

JOLLY ROGER

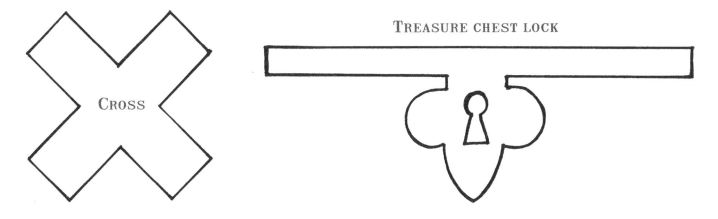

CROSS

TREASURE CHEST LOCK

TREASURE ISLAND MAP

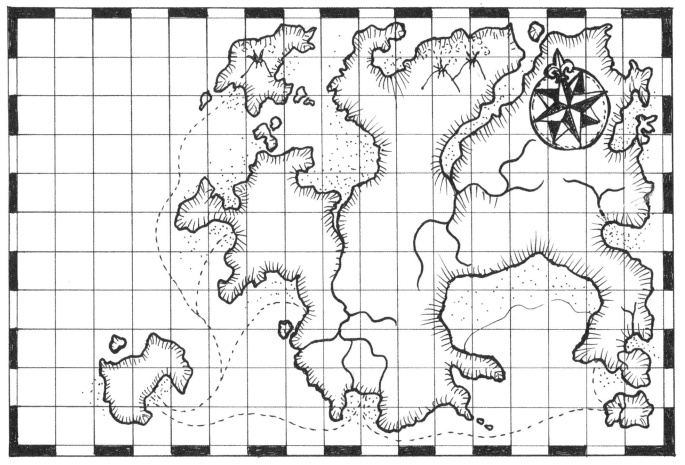

1 square = 10cm square

TREES, CLOUDS, BIRDS, WOODLAND CREATURES AND PUMPKINS
for Felt Forest pages 74–79

Copy all the pieces at 100%

TUMBLING BOOS
*for Tumbling Boo Building
Blocks pages 80-83*

Copy all the outlines at 100%

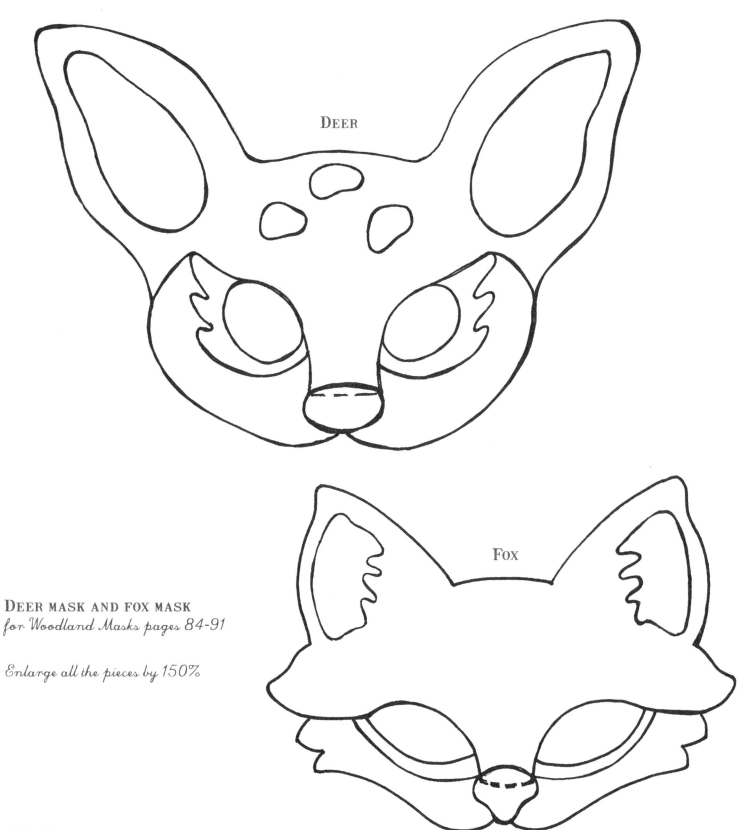

DEER

FOX

DEER MASK AND FOX MASK
for Woodland Masks pages 84-91

Enlarge all the pieces by 150%

OWL

SQUIRREL

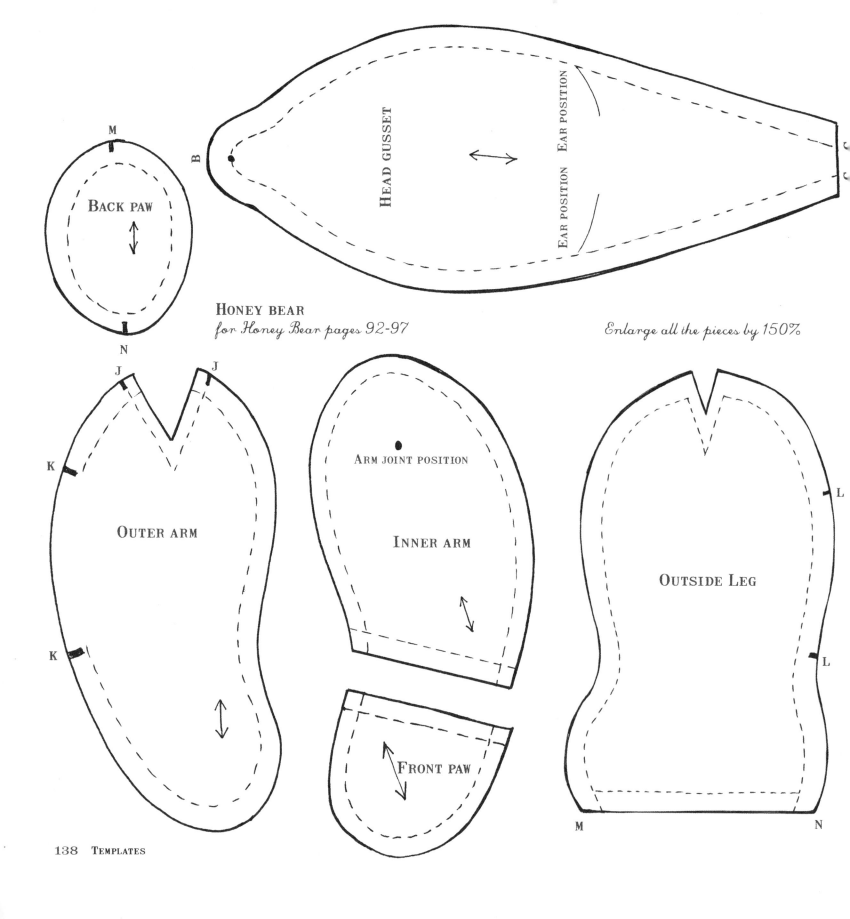

M

BACK PAW

B

HEAD GUSSET

EAR POSITION

EAR POSITION

C

C

N

HONEY BEAR
for Honey Bear pages 92–97

Enlarge all the pieces by 150%

J   J

K

OUTER ARM

K

ARM JOINT POSITION

INNER ARM

L

OUTSIDE LEG

L

FRONT PAW

M   N

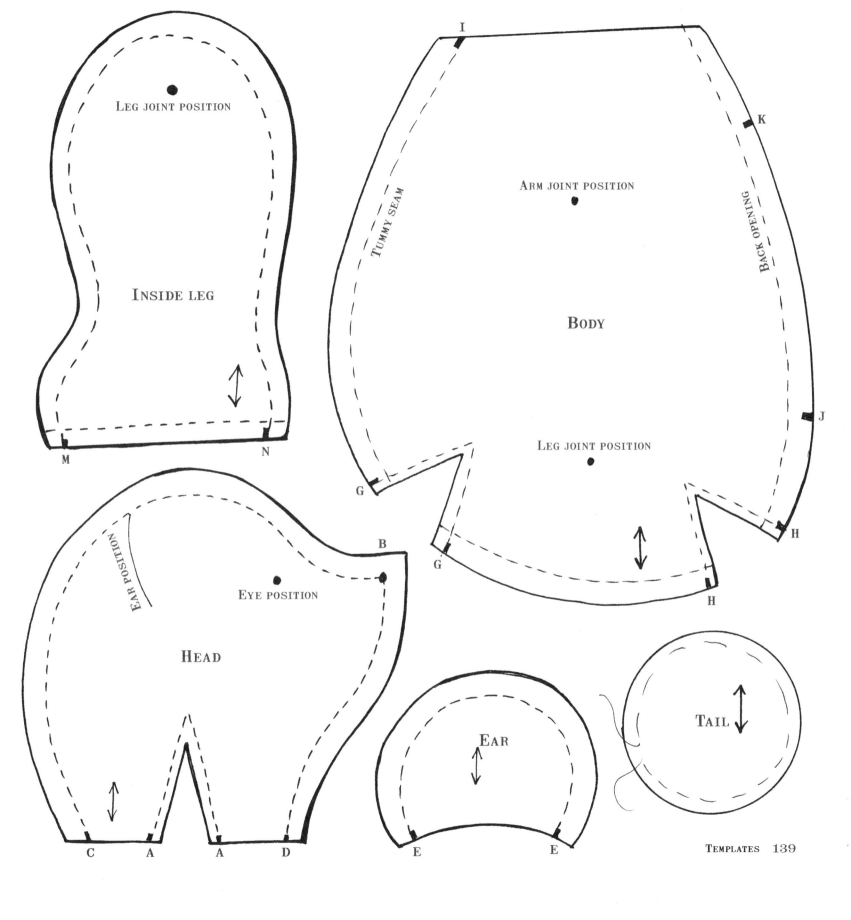

INSIDE LEG

Leg joint position

M

N

BODY

TUMMY SEAM

BACK OPENING

ARM JOINT POSITION

Leg joint position

I

K

J

G

H

HEAD

EAR POSITION

EYE POSITION

B

G

H

C

A

A

D

EAR

E

E

TAIL

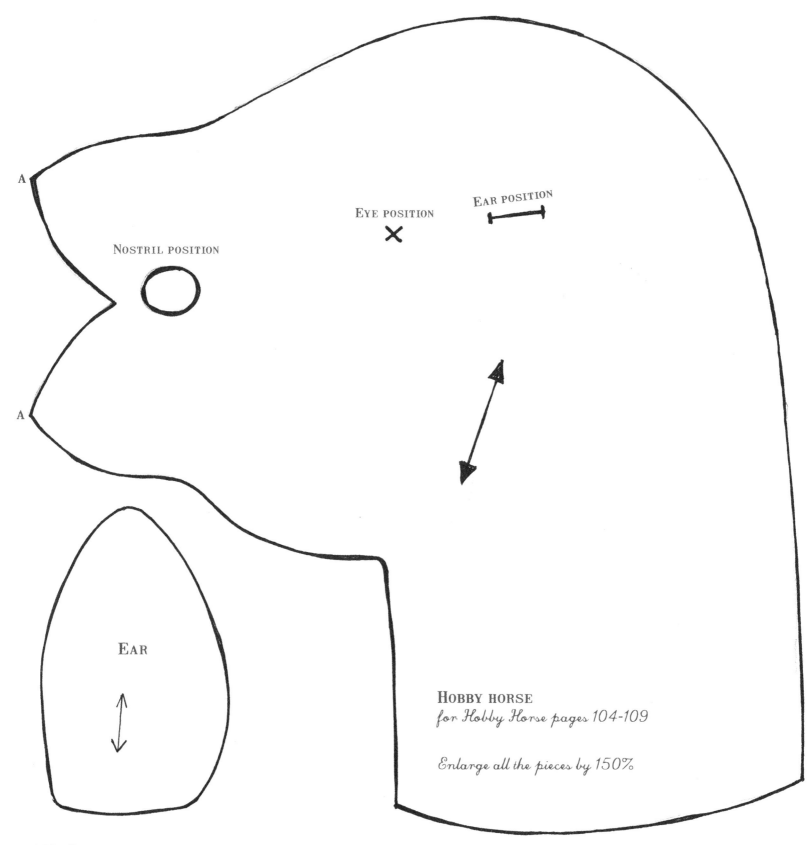

A

Nostril position

A

Eye position

×

Ear position

Ear

Hobby horse
for Hobby Horse pages 104-109

Enlarge all the pieces by 150%

NUMERALS
for Advent Calendar pages 114-119

1234
567
890

BOO
for Christmas Ornaments pages 110-113

Copy all the pieces at 100%

Suppliers

BELLE & BOO
0117 924 6382
hello@belleandboo.com
www.belleandboo.com

CLOTH HOUSE
47 Berwick Street
London W1F 8SJ
020 7437 5155
info@clothhouse.com
www.clothhouse.net

DMC CREATIVE WORLD
Unit 22 Warren Park Way
Warrens Park
Leicester LE19 4SA
0116 275 4000
www.dmccreative.co.uk

E-CRAFTS
Stocks: safety toy eyes and joints.
sales@e-crafts.co.uk
www.e-crafts.co.uk

FABRIC LAND
Branches in Basingstoke, Brighton,
Bristol, Bournemouth, Kingston,
Portsmouth, Reading, Salisbury
and Southampton
www.fabricland.co.uk

HARTS OF HERTFORD
14 Bull Plain
Hertford SG14 1DT
01992 558 106
info@hartsofhertford.co.uk
www.hartsofhertford.co.uk

HOBBYCRAFT
0330 026 1400
www.hobbycraft.co.uk

JOHN LEWIS
Stocks: fabrics and haberdashery.
Oxford Street
London W1A 1EX
and branches nationwide
08456 049 049
www.johnlewis.com

KLEINS
5 Noel Street
London W1F 8GD
020 7437 6162
kleins@kleins.co.uk
www.kleins.co.uk

MacCULLOCH & WALLIS
25–26 Dering Street
London W1S 1AT
020 7629 0311
mailorder@macculloch.com
www.macculloch-wallis.co.uk

THE MAKERY
Beau Nash House
19 Union Passage
Bath, Avon BA1 1RD
01225 581 888
alice@themakery.co.uk
www.themakery.co.uk

MANDORS
134 Renfrew Street
Glasgow G3 6ST
0141 332 7716
fabric@mandors.co.uk
www.mandors.co.uk

MILLIE MOON
24–25 Catherine Hill
Frome, Somerset BA11 1BY
01373 464 650
info@milliemoonshop.co.uk
www.milliemoonshop.co.uk

MOHAIR BEAR MAKING SUPPLIES
Stocks: safety toy eyes and joints.
Unit 3, Horton Court
Hortonwood 50
Telford, Shropshire TF1 7GY
01952 604 096
sales@mohairbearmakingsupplies.co.uk
www.mohairbearmakingsupplies.co.uk

NUTSCENE
Stocks: Nutscene jute 3-ply garden twine.
01307 468 589
sales@nutscene.com
www.nutscene.com

PAPER AND STRING
Stocks: Felt, ribbon and button.
01308 898 239
www.paper-and-string.co.uk

TIKKI
Stocks: fabric, felt and ric rac.
293 Sandycombe Road,
Kew Gardens,
London TW9 3LU
020 8948 8462
info@tikkilondon.com
www.tikkilondon.com

WOODWORKS CRAFT SUPPLIES
Stocks: wooden eggs.
www.woodworkscraftsupplies.co.uk

WOOL AND FELT
Stocks: coloured felt.
01981 540 470
www.woolandfelt.co.uk

WOOL FELT COMPANY
Stocks: coloured felt.
www.woolfeltcompany.co.uk

Index

PROJECTS CONCEIVED AND MADE BY
Lucinda Ganderton and Lisa Pendreigh

PUBLISHING DIRECTOR Jane O'Shea
COMMISSIONING EDITOR Lisa Pendreigh
CREATIVE DIRECTOR Helen Lewis
ART DIRECTION AND DESIGN Claire Peters
ILLUSTRATOR Mandy Sutcliffe
PHOTOGRAPHER Laura Edwards
STYLIST Polly Webb-Wilson
MODELS Charlie Weeks, Meadow Nobrega
and Dulcie Nobrega at Bruce and Brown, and
Teddy Read-Baldrey
PRODUCTION DIRECTOR Vincent Smith
PRODUCTION CONTROLLER Emily Noto

Quadrille
craft

www.quadrillecraft.com

First published in 2015 by
Quadrille Publishing Ltd
Pentagon House
52–54 Southwark Street
London SE1 1UN
www.quadrille.co.uk

Quadrille is an imprint of Hardie Grant.
www.hardiegrant.com.au

If you have any comments or
queries regarding the instructions
in this book, please contact us at
enquiries@quadrille.co.uk

British Library Cataloguing-in-Publication Data.
A catalogue record for this book is available from the
British Library.

ISBN: 978 184949 588 2

Printed in China